SINTOWN SAINTS

The Bordeaux's

From the South Side to the West Coast

6/25/2020

Holly:

Thank You For

the Support

Jacq Bordeaux

Jacques Bordeaux

outskirts
press

TABLE OF CONTENTS

This book is dedicated in equal and infinite measure to Daddy, Momma and Valerie.

FOREWORD

IT WAS 2010 and I was returning home from a business trip looking forward to some down time. Then, I considered my cellphone a necessary irritant. As I checked my messages I saw a text from Jacques Bordeaux. I quickly scanned the text to assure it was not an emergency. As I read Jacques text, I was struck by the loving and straightforward prose that soared above the usual inanities occupied by the digital green bubbles. Not here. Not this text. As I continued reading I was transported from my overly-scheduled world to lyrical prose filled with unconditional love. Who knew that first missive from my "ace boon" would eventually become this fantastic memoir--Sintown Saints.

I sent that original text to friends and associates as a demonstration of the power of bearing witness to our aging parents or any loved ones. Everyone I sent it to commented on how moving it was that Jacques thumbed out extraordinary reflections and observations while sitting with his dad, Clovis Bordeaux, as he bore witness to his transition from here to there. Jacques prose was straightforward yet elegant, deeply felt yet measured, and compelling yet observant.

Sintown Saints gives us all the opportunity to be transported again and again. This collection of vignettes takes us through the Bordeaux family's personal journey during important milestones in our country's history. Jacques reminds us of our adolescent obsessions with comic books and bicycles while also telling hard truths about racism and its impact on us all.

Beginning with those initial thumb taps at his Dad's bedside recounting his blessings, Sintown Saints is a gift Jacques has bestowed upon all that seek humanity, dignity of spirit and unconditional love. Enjoy this wonderful work.

James Bell
San Francisco

PREFACE

SINTOWN SAINTS IS a book about blessings large and small. I have lived a blessed existence. I was born into a home with two parents. Both were educated and decidedly upwardly mobile. Daddy was a black scientist—a physicist—at a time when there wasn't such a thing. Momma was a third-grade teacher, who taught in five cities across three states. They maintained an almost military order and structure in our home that the four of us children tested at every opportunity with varying degrees of success.

My three brothers, Sammy, Jude, and Visey were and are rock-steady blessings in my life. I'm the youngest and had the benefit of their examples to emulate. In some instances, they provided great lessons on what *not* to do. We were growing up in the turbulent 50s and 60s, and we were a vocal and rambunctious bunch. Our dinner table was polite and ordered; we mostly waited to be spoken to before speaking, but decorum could not keep the news of the day from seeping into our dinner conversations. Our parents' willingness to let us discuss, debate and argue the actions and personalities of the burgeoning Civil Rights movement was a blessing. We learned a lot of uncomfortable lessons about Plessy and Marshall and the NAACP and King and Malcolm and Bull Connor and George Wallace and Dixiecrats and lynching and Selma and Montgomery around our dinner table.

Education and an innate love of learning was one of my biggest blessings. Momma and Daddy made sure we were well-read and well-rounded. We all attended Catholic schools wherever we lived. Momma bought us collections of the "100 Greatest" everything: novels; American songs; paintings and anything else she thought might uplift us in our home. We took trips to museums and stage plays, and Momma dressed us in suits and ties *whenever* we went out in public. We spoke proper English, and I paid a social price for that—often being accused of "trying to act White." My brothers and I learned to manipulate and shade the language to suit the occasion. This skill has allowed me to speak to family, friends, and colleagues clearly and effectively, regardless of the circumstance. I had a set of live-in tutors who introduced me to the newest slang and sayings of the day and allowed me to dip into colloquialisms and popular references whenever the need arose. Momma thought slang was an abomination: the language of hoodlums, thugs, and heathens; but what a blessing!

I am the beneficiary of the struggles of Black Americans who came before me. I was born one year before Rosa Parks refused to give up her seat in the front of the bus and Thurgood Marshall argued Brown v Board of Education in front of the Warren Supreme Court. Momma and Daddy put themselves in a position to get the jobs and buy the homes that housed my childhood and adolescence. I always had my own bed and shared my bedroom with only one of my brothers. I was always sure about my next meal. I had a bike just like my brothers, and a car too. After we moved from Chicago to Compton to Pomona, I had a pool in my backyard. Compared to the overwhelming majority of Black people in this country, I have lived a charmed and blessed life. I am very cognizant of these blessings and am thankful for them.

The focus on Sintown as a place is important. As part of the Great Migration of African American famililies from the South and MidWest to the North and West, our family went from the South Side of Chicago to Compton and then Pomona, California. When we finally landed in Pomona, Momma and Daddy were only shown houses in specific parts of town; mainly those neighborhoods that immediately surrounded the city's three high schools. These were red-lined enclaves where Negroes were congregated. We joined families from Florida, Georgia, Missouri, Texas, Alabama and Louisiana and settled into these neighborhoods, made friends and got involved in the life of the hood. For the young people that I knew, Sintown, the name given to the suburban tract neighborhoods around Ganesha High School, was home. Often, two or three branches of a family would own homes in Sintown. One couple accepted six nieces and nephews from Louisiana when their parents tragically died. Bonds were formed around the high school's sports teams and other extra-currilulars. Without intentionally doing so, we formed a community that produced what I refer to as Saints: people who were there for me in any number of situations. Parents, brothers, friends, teachers and a bunch of other adults and elders who gave of themselves to enrich my life. Sintown Saints.

My father once sat me down and told me why he was so adamant that I get an education and make something of myself. His father died in 1934 when Daddy was not yet seventeen. As the oldest child, he became the de facto man of the house for his six brothers and sisters. He had come of age in the heart of the Great Depression and his family was shattered. His mother, though trained as a teacher, could not get a job teaching because the superintendent of St. Louis Schools said women who were wives could not teach in the district. She said she was a widow, not a wife. The superintendent would not relent. Daddy's mother put his three sisters in an orphanage because there was not enough money to support all of her children. Her brother, Donald, stepped up to help out, even on his Postal Service salary. Uncle Don paid much of Daddy's tuition to Lincoln University as well as that of brother Donald and sister Elizabeth; he helped other siblings with car down-payments and, in at least two instances, paid for house downs outright. In Daddy's eyes, Uncle Don was the salt of the earth and the bar against which everyone else, man or woman, was measured. Daddy then told me, "I'm going to give you what my father and Uncle Don gave me and I'll add a little something to it. I expect you to give your kids what I've given you and add a little something to it." This belief was his way of saying his life had been infinitely better than the life his parents had because of the help Uncle Don and others had given him and his siblings, and he was determined to give my brothers and me the same leg up he had received. His message was simple: You must be educated and prepared to pass the family blessings on.

But with a lot of blessings come a lot of responsibilities. I have felt an enormous responsibility to live up to the model set forth by Momma and Daddy. I got a college degree because that's what Momma and Daddy expected of me—and my brothers. When I was growing up, 'where' to get it was the only part I had a voice in deciding. My parents were ready and able to pay for our education out of pocket. We understood that we must complete college on our way to making whatever contribution we were going to make.

Momma and Daddy married in 1947 and were together until Momma passed. Daddy kissed her picture every day after her passing until he could no longer manage. "Neecy" was his everything. I have tried my best to emulate that dedication to spouse and family. To date, my wife, Valerie, and I have been married for forty-three years and counting. Providing a solid home for our kids, Mike, Sarai, and Imani (the best damn kids there ever were) was the least I was called upon to do. Earning a decent living and making a mark in my field were givens.

So here we are. This book has been a kind of 'continuing education' for me. I have sorted a few things out and come to understand the road I have walked and how blessed and fortunate I have been. The telling of stories and the remembering of people, places, and events in our family are lessons I cherish. And this is mainly for my children. I want to give them a sense of where they come from, at least on the Perkins-Bordeaux side of our family. The joy, grit, and humanity I see in them comes in equal measure from Valerie and me. But I can trace so much of it right back to Clovis and Bernice and the rest of our extended family.

AND THAT'S HOW I GOT MY SCAR

WHEN MOMMA AND Daddy told us their plans for the evening, I saw Sammy and Jude glance at one another, and their faces had a look of poorly hidden mischief. Momma said she and Daddy were going out. Momma wanted to hear some music; Daddy said they might go see a movie. In any event, he said they would be home around eleven and that Sammy, being the oldest, would be in charge. Now Sammy and Jude were rivals of the

The Bordeaux Boys: Sammy, Jude Visey and me.

first order, and normally, this would have sent Jude, who was only eleven months younger, over the moon. But those two were in cahoots and ready to put a plan of their own into motion. Next in order of leadership succession came Clovis, Jr.—whom everybody called Visey—but he, like me, probably didn't care because he was way interested in what might be up after our parents left. Being four years younger, I was in effect, the "baby" everybody else had to keep an eye on. It wasn't that I was clumsy or accident-prone; stuff just happened to me. Of course, it didn't help that my brothers saw me as their live-in guinea pig. "If there was something my brothers were reluctant to try, they experimented on me. I was the kid in the LIFE Cereal Commercial. Back in the day, there was a television commercial where two mischievous brothers conspire to feed this cereal to an unsuspecting baby brother. They say, "Let's get Mikey. He'll hate it; he hates everything!" I was the opposite: if I liked something, Sammy, Jude, and Visey would try it.

It turns out that Jude had overheard Momma and Daddy making their date plans and had gone to Sammy to start devising their plot. There would be Motown records and dance steps taught by Jude, the coolest brother; scary movies on TV and popcorn with hot sauce; tag-team wrestling on the fold-out bed in the basement; target shooting with the BB gun; and, all the penny-candy we could eat. The two older boys had started using their allowance money to stockpile the red licorice shoestrings, wax lips, and candy dots to fuel the festivities. Visey and I sensed that something cool was afoot, but we were not in on the planning because we surely would have spilled the beans.

This Friday, like all Friday afternoons, after depositing their paychecks and getting home from work, Momma and Daddy set the table in record time. Because of what day it was in our

Catholic home, Daddy had picked up fried fish and fries at the "You Buy, We Fry" joint he hit on the way home. I watched Momma and Daddy as they danced around our small kitchen. In a flash, the catfish was on a plate in the middle of the table. Momma grabbed the coleslaw she had put together the night before and a jar of dill pickle slices out of the fridge and spun both like tops into perfect position on either side of the fish. Before the door of the fridge could close, she returned for the ketchup and hot sauce. Daddy pivoted around the counter, grabbed six plates out of the cabinet, and reverse-pivoted to deposit them on the table. Daddy had once been a waiter on the Mississippi Riverboats docked at St. Louis and could set a table in microseconds. After he had dealt the plates like cards, he turned and reached over the counter, flicked open the silverware drawer, and grabbed exactly six forks and a tablespoon. He closed the drawer with his left hand, turned, forked every plate and spooned the slaw. Then he inspected his effort and looked at Momma. She winked and nodded almost imperceptibly. He announced, "Dinner's on the table!" in a voice that carried throughout the house. Sammy and Jude were down in the basement. Visey was in the bedroom with his comic books. Still, Daddy got the requisite "Yessir!" from each of us. We knew when he called us to the table that meant he was ready to eat. None of us wanted to keep Daddy waiting, especially if there was food involved.

Jude and Sammy seemed to magically appear at the table. They were hyper-cooperative 'cause they wanted Momma and Daddy out of the house faster than our parents wanted to leave. When Visey and I did not similarly appear, Momma called, "NOW, Please!" Once we had taken our seats, Daddy said the blessing. I was always struck by how grateful Daddy

was, and his recited blessing of our food reflected that grati-
tude. However, once he finished, he dug in. Daddy was served
first, followed by Momma, Sammy, and so on down the line.
Needless to say, there wasn't jack left for Jacques by the time
the various plates got around to me. But Daddy was the food
sheriff and made sure I got a decent serving. Before long, we
were crunching and munching on fish and fries and pickles
and coleslaw. Momma remembered some bottles of root beer
and cream soda in the fridge. She grabbed three and popped
them open. She retrieved six plastic tumblers and passed them
around. The four of us were root beer guys, but Momma and
Daddy were brown cream soda folks from way back.

Dinner was over quickly, and we knew the drill. Daddy and
Momma had retreated into their boudoir to get ready, and we
knew what to do: Clear the table, wipe everything down, put
everything away, wash the dishes, put away the dishes. Sammy
immediately plugged the sink and began running dishwater.
Visey collected all the dishes and carried them over to Sammy's
sink. I got the tumblers and Jude got the silverware. We
dumped them into the sink and Jude grabbed and wrung out a
dish towel. While he began with the counter, Visey scooped up
the condiments and coleslaw and crammed them into empty
spaces in the fridge. Jude moved nimbly to the table and wiped
it completely clean in a matter of seconds. Visey and I dragged
chairs around to face the cabinets and climbed atop them. Jude
began rinsing and drying the dishes and handing them to Visey
and me. As we got down to the silverware, I dragged the chairs
back to the table. By the time Momma and Daddy came out
of the bedroom, the kitchen was clean and ready for inspection. The closer they got to the front door, the more giddiness
Sammy and Jude had to suppress.

SINTOWN SAINTS

Finally, the door closed behind Daddy. Ever the gentleman, Daddy held the door open for Momma with a deep and elaborate bow, and she responded with the exaggerated stride of the upper-crust, "Hoity-Toity" they both ridiculed at every opportunity. Visey ran into Jude and Sammy's room and instantly emerged with a small stack of 45s. He had the yellow whatchamacallit that went in the middle of the record between his teeth.

Now, we were about to play music on Daddy's Hi-Fi. This audio altar was his pride and joy. The Hi-Fi was a practical application of his electrical and engineering skills residing in a cabinet he had designed and assembled. He painted it with red cherry-wood stain that accentuated the grain of the wood he used. The cabinet held a receiver, an amplifier, a turntable and The *piece de resistance*—the speakers. Daddy had selected and installed them. When he played his Ellington or Momma's Ella records on this marvel, you could feel the pride in his craftsmanship, his engineering knowledge. And we were about to desecrate this masterpiece with our little 45s.

The first one Visey put on was "Get a Job" by The Miracles. The way Visey talked about the group's leader, Smokey Robinson, you woulda thought he was the greatest singer-songwriter ever. What followed was a Motown on Parade. Martha Reeves, the Supremes, the Four Tops, and the Temptations. The Temptations were Jude's absolute favorite. He liked their sound, with David Ruffin and Eddie Kendrick's crooning. But he also liked their style. He dug the suits, the patent-leather shoes, the tuxedo-style shirts, the processed hair. Jude was not unusual in this regard. But what he truly loved were their dance moves. When Visey played a Temptation tune, Jude started stepping to the music. Visey and Sammy fell in behind him and stepped, just as we had seen the Temps do when they were on the Ed Sullivan Show. I jumped in and got hopelessly lost in the music. Thankfully, my two left feet didn't stop the next great Motown group from stopping the show.

All of a sudden, Sammy broke ranks, ran through the kitchen and down the stairs to the basement. He threw the cushions off the fold-out sofa Daddy had stashed down there. He yanked the bed open and started bouncing on it like a trampoline. Time for some tag-team wrestling. He immediately picked Visey, which meant that Jude got me by default. We were now the wrestling teams that squared off for epic re-enactments of the Friday Night Wrestling we waited all week to watch. Headlocks and leg locks. Full- and half-Nelsons. It's a miracle somebody didn't bump their head on the bed frame, the way we were jumping around.

After everyone had used me as their wrestling dummy, Visey ran back upstairs to the kitchen. We knew what was happening up there when we heard the familiar clang and bang of the popcorn pots. We all ran up and by the time I got there, Sammy and Jude were in a pitched battle over the proper popcorn condiments. Jude was a traditional butter and salt popcorn eater. He actually made the best popcorn in the house. He was precise with his Crisco to kernel ratio. His cooking flame was just right for a consistent pop. He covered the pan and shook it gently and steadily throughout the popping process. He was simpatico with the kernels and coaxed them to the height of fluffy poppiness. Of course he would want only sweet butter and a gentle sprinkling of salt on them.

Sammy, on the other hand, wanted lots and lots and lots of hot sauce. Whenever we went to the drive-in, Sammy would have his own bag of Red Rooster popcorn. But this night, he was claiming the butter made the popcorn greasy. Jude said the hot sauce made the popcorn soggy and nasty. Visey and I were in the peanut gallery testifying. We both loved Jude's popcorn but had to admit the hot sauce was tasty in moderation. We proposed this compromise to both sides and arrived at an equitable settlement. Jude would get his butter and salt; Sammy would get seven shakes of the hot sauce bottle. He had started out at fifteen shakes but we talked him down. We broke out another root beer and passed it around. Sammy ran into the room he shared with Jude and emerged with red shoestring licorice for everybody. Visey went into the living room and put on another record. He turned the volume up and "The way you do the thing you do!" bounced off of every wall in the house. The four of us sat around the kitchen table, laughing at each other and singing along.

Visey jumped up and ran back down in the basement yelling, "I'M FIRST!" He grabbed the BB gun Daddy had given us and slowly started pouring the BB's down the barrel. Sammy and Jude hung the green army blanket on which Daddy had spray-painted a fluorescent yellow target. I had gone to pee before going downstairs. Just as I hit the last three steps, I saw Visey coming at me. He was holding the BB gun up in his right hand, and before I knew it, the end of the barrel caught me right below my left eyebrow. I fell back on the stairs and grabbed my forehead. The rifle sight had smacked the bone of my eye socket and I knew I had been hit. It hurt, but not that much. I didn't, however, know I was bleeding. The palm of my hand was wet with more blood than I had ever seen. I went OFF! In seconds, I was screaming and rocking back and forth on the stairs. Sammy and Jude had run over as soon as they heard me. One said, "Oh, SHIT!" The other told Visey that

Momma was going to kill him.

Jude ran to the bathroom and got a towel. He wet it and pressed it onto my face. Sammy got all bug-eyed when he saw that Jude had grabbed one of Momma's good towels. He started rattling on about us having to throw the towel away so Momma woudn't find it; like she wasn't going to notice the hole in her son's head. Jude ignored Sammy and went back to the bathroom to rinse the towel. This time, he wiped my face off and cleaned up the residual blood. He went back to the bathroom one more time, and this time, he brought a couple of Band-Aids. He put one over the cut, and I just knew it made me look tougher than my seven-year-old self.

Visey went and removed any evidence that we had had hands on Daddy's Hi-Fi. Sammy swept through the kitchen, cleaning up after the popcorn. Jude went downstairs and took down the army blanket and put the sofa back together. I was starting to get a headache, so I went into our room and climbed into my top bunk. I had to sleep on my right side because of my injury. I fell asleep dreamimg of being Mr. Cool, a super-spy with an eyepatch.

I snapped awake when I heard Daddy's keys land loudly in the orange art-deco glass bowl on the table next to the door. It took me a minute to think why I had a band-aid over my eye. Just as I remembered the barrel of the BB gun, Momma opened the door to my room. She turned on the light and scanned the room. She looked at Visey in the bottom bunk. I've always thought that Momma could sense that something wasn't right because she started walking toward me with her head cocked. When she saw the Band-Aid, her curiosity and anger crystallized into the need for an instant explanation.

"Jacques Phillipe Bordeaux! What happened to your face?"

"I don't know! I was just running down the stairs and Visey hit me!"

Visey heard this and exploded from his faked slumber. He started reliving the entire episode in thirty seconds and a single breath. He must have said the word 'accident' seventeen times. By now, Daddy, Jude, and Sammy had appeared at the door. Jude pretty much vouched for everything Visey had said. It was the first time I ever heard someone use the term, "wrong place, wrong time."

Momma had calmed down and started looking closely at her little boy. She smiled at me and shook her head. "You're just an accident waiting to happen, aren't you?"

"Yes'm."

Momma didn't even acknowledge my response because her eyes were fixed now on Visey. He had thought because Momma rushed to see about me, his part in this misadventure was somehow overlooked. As soon as he saw Momma's eyes locked on him, he knew he was not long for this world. She said, "Clovis."

In our house, there were gradations to Momma's anger, and we measured it by how many of your names she used. In Visey's case, she used his proper name and not his nickname. If she had used "CLOVIS ALONZO BORDEAUX, JR." he would have known he was a goner. So, when Momma said just his first name, he was sure he could endure this trial. She asked him to explain, calmly, what had happened. Visey tried to recall what details he had blurted out before so as not to contradict himself. All he really came up with was, "It was an accident."

"Were you running on the stairs?"

"Yes Ma'am." He quickly thought better, "No…No Ma'am!"

"Which is it"

"Well, I was starting to run, but I wasn't really on the stairs so, technically, I wasn't running *ON* the stairs."

"You think this is funny?"

"No, no, no. I was saying that I would never run *ON* the stairs, so. . ."

"Where were you taking the BB gun? Didn't Daddy tell you to leave it in the basement?" The fact that Visey had violated a Daddy rule was serious.

"Yes Ma'am."

"So where were you taking it as you weren't running up the stairs?"

"Nowhere."

At this point, Visey could see the offenses piling up against him, and he might as well end this before Momma started getting into three-name angry territory. He could see the whupping in his future, but he was hoping that Momma's heart wasn't really in it. She told me to get up and get in the bed with Daddy. "Close the door as you leave."

We all knew what to expect from a whupping. Our parents used them to punish up to a certain age. They wanted to give us something to think about that next time whatever stupidity put us there cropped up. Momma was not a "This is going to hurt me more than it hurts you," kind of person. She was going to punish you as she had been punished by her parents, Van and Sarah.

What I heard coming from the bedroom I shared with Visey was not Momma screaming and swinging followed by Visey crying and swearing not to do whatever he did again. Her voice was clear and hard.

"Your accident hurt my baby!"

"I didn't mean to!"

"Be quiet when I'm talking to you!"

"Sammy and Jude were running, too!"

"I'm not talking to them. I'm talking to you!"

"It was an accident!"

When Momma had heard that word enough, she slapped Visey. The sound of her hand on his head was sharp. I know Visey wasn't expecting it.

"What would you have done if your "accident" had done real damage?"

"He wasn't hurt that bad." I could hear Visey's voice starting to crack.

She slapped him again. This one sounded harder.

"You're supposed to take care of your brother. That's why I'm so mad at you."

"I'm sorry," Visey said, hoping to get Momma to stop hitting him.

"We trusted you to take care of each other."

"I'm sorry," he said again.

"Don't be sorry. Take better care of your brother next time."

"I will."

I went back to my room and heard Visey breathing irregularly with his head under the covers. I climbed up into the top bunk and pulled the covers up to my chin. By now, the pain in my eye was just a dull reminder. Momma had returned to her bedroom, but she and Daddy didn't go to sleep for a long time. I could tell they were talking about Visey, cause about all I heard Momma say was, "That boy..."

CHORES

"The work's not done 'til the last man falls."
Bernice, c. 1961

SATURDAY CHORES WERE a given when we were boys. You could sneak in a Saturday cartoon or two and maybe a bowl of cereal if you got up early enough. But you knew the TV went off at an appropriate time and then... IT was on. In our home, grass had to be cut, car(s) had to be washed and vacuumed, floors had to mopped, bathrooms had to be cleaned, beds made and bedrooms straightened,

Momma was in charge when it came to chores.

trash emptied, groceries bought, groceries put away, baths taken, clothes laid out for Sunday Mass, etc. In other words, there was enough work to keep everyone busy for most of the day.

There was no discussion about the appropriateness of a given chore. It was Saturday—ergo, chores. Momma was in charge of this production. She decided on the prioritization, who was assigned what, and most importantly, when a chore could be declared finished. She insisted on the generous application of "elbow grease," or, "scrubbing, not rubbing." Her inspections were pretty simple and straightforward; if she didn't like it, you did it over. Real simple.

Daddy liked an orderly house. Momma liked a clean house. I think they liked us working as a group just as much. Daddy especially liked us cooperating with one another: A unit; a team. It was sort of informal because everyone understood the objective. There was always music in the background. Ella or Ellington, Wes Montgomery or Basie. Momma would sing along. "a tisket, a tasket . . ." Sometimes they played classical, though I can't tell you who or what.

Needless to say, allowances were bound to chores. Chores were not linked or tied to our allowances; they were welded, lashed, bound like a Gordian Knot. It started generally. If you did chores to Momma and Daddy's expectations, you got allowance. I don't even remember how much we got. There's an urban myth in my memory that Momma and Daddy wanted each of us to get a quarter allowance every week. The first week we were to receive our quarters, Momma gave Sammy a dollar and told him to go down to the corner store, get change and give each brother his quarter. Momma gave Sammy the dollar on Friday. On Sunday, Daddy asked Jude how he spent his quarter. Jude said, "What quarter?"

When Daddy explained the quarter-a-week-allowance plan, Jude and Visey went ballistic. They looked at Sammy, and all he could muster was this Alfred E. "Newman-esque" grin. Newman was the gap-toothed, Howdy Doody-looking character that appeared on the cover of every MAD Magazine. Sammy got in so many different levels of trouble with this episode, with Momma yelling, "You must have lost your mind!" Daddy reached for the belt and deliverd a well-deserved whuppin'. Jude and Visey wanted to add their two cents, suggesting that they should get Sammy's quarter next week. When I realized what was going on, I just saw a lot of penny candy and comic books in my future.

Later, Daddy tried to inject some entrepreneurial incentives by putting a dollar value on each chore. With four boys in the house, competition would flourish, everyone would earn something, and all the chores would get done. Everybody wins. I even remember a chart with chores from small to large with commensurate amounts attached. Sammy and Visey seemed okay with it, but Jude balked. His thinking was that since you chose what chores to do, you could, in theory, choose to do no chores at all.

When it was time for the Saturday cartoons to be switched off, Visey and I got our chore-play clothes on and cleaned our room, trying to look busy. Sammy and Jude shared the other bedroom in our house. Both rooms had a bunk-bed set with matching dresser and desk. Sammy finished cleaning his side of their room and then went to clean a bathroom. Jude climbed into the top bunk bed and started reading a comic book.

Clothes had to be picked up and put away or put in the dirty clothes bag. Our beds had to be stripped and re-made. This task was no easy feat for two little kids wrestling with bunk-bed mattresses. The dirty sheets had to go down to the washer-dryer in the basement. General mess had to be straightened out. Keeping our bedroom clean was usually not a problem 'cause, for Visey and me, our room was our display space. Our model car masterpieces posed on the dresser, and WWII fighter jets like the ones Daddy worked on with the "Airmen" hung from the ceiling. Our covers might not have been straight, but the room was clean. We'd pass Bernice's inspection.

When we finished, we ran down the hall to Sammy and Jude's room. We heard the tinny sound of "You've Really Got a Hold on Me" coming from Jude's transistor radio and noticed that Sammy's bottom bunk was neatly made and everything that was his was where it was supposed to be. Jude was laying in his bed, listening to the radio, reading a comic book and working on a Big Hunk candy bar. His bed had not been touched and his school uniform pants still hung on the bedpost from after school on Friday. There was a bath towel on the floor, and his school shoes sat where they landed when he kicked them off the day before. Visey glared at Jude and yelled in a whisper that he better get out of that bed and get to work like the rest of us. "You're gonna get us all in trouble! Momma's going to KILL you. And then she's gonna have Daddy kill you again!" Jude ignored him. I figured this would last right up until Momma saw Jude lounging on an official Saturday Chore Day. I also started thinking about what Jude-chores I could do and maybe earn a little more candy and comic book money.

Sammy came in the room and stated flatly that he already tried to talk sense to Jude. "He's just being ignorant. He thinks Momma and Daddy are just going to let him not do chores. When was the last time someone around here didn't do chores?" Jude interrupted. "If Momma wants to pay me for my chores, fine. But if I choose not to do chores, leave me alone." I blurted out, "What are you gonna do when you don't have any money 'cause you didn't do no chores?" "When I need the money, I'll do the chores," Jude explained.

Visey was getting visibly perturbed about this. "You're not the only one who's going to get in trouble. Momma will be mad all day, and she's gonna nit-pick everything. I'ma have to vacuum the living room three times. Sammy turned and headed out of the room. "I don't want to be anywhere nearby when Momma and Daddy see this." Visey and I followed. We figured cleaning the basement was a three-kid job where we could ride out the coming storm.

Momma and Daddy had run over to St. Joachim's for some kind of meeting. They said they would be back by ten o'clock. Visey started counting down when he heard the key in the front door lock. "Ten-nine-eight. . ." Momma's voice laughing at something Clo had said. "Seven-six-five. . ." Daddy's keys clinking in the glass bowl by the door "Four-three-two. . ." "God bless the child. . ." "One."

"WHAT DO YOU THINK YOU ARE DOING?" Sammy, Visey and I looked at one another and realized we were definitely going to get swept up in whatever would happen that day. We scrambled up the stairs to witness the battle of wills.

"Are all your chores done? Why are you in the bed? Are you sick? Did you hurt yourself?" Both Daddy and Momma were in the room. Momma shot rapid-fire questions at Jude. These questions caught him off guard. He was expecting a more reasoned, Clovis-style conversation about chores and their value. Instead, he got vintage Neecy. Jude stammered, "I don't care about getting paid. I just don't want to do any chores." Momma laughed, "I don't care about you getting paid either, so you won't be." "You're a little confused, son." Daddy said. "You live here; you do chores. The allowance is gravy." Momma was warming up. "As a matter of fact, you should be paying us to live here."

By this time, Jude was kneeling in his top bunk, realizing that he was quickly losing this particular chess match. He argued that since they were willing to pay for individual chores, he could decide which, if any, chores he would do. He was looking straight at me and Visey and Sammy as if we were a jury of his peers that supported this nonsense. Sammy just shook his head. None of us wanted to be on this particular team.

Clo told Jude he had about three seconds to get out of that bed and get to work. This had been a nice conversation, but there was work to do. Momma calmed down for a minute and talked to Jude like he was one of her third-grade students, "We want to pay you so you will have some walking-around money. That has nothing to do with you doing, or not doing, chores. We give you a bed, food, clothes, toys, books, and a lot of other stuff. Doing chores is how you pitch in; how you help out." We marveled at how calm Bernice was. She was asthmatic, and when she got worked up, she would start wheezing and coughing and reaching for her atomizer. There was none of that.

I expected Jude to climb out of bed and join us in Choreville, but he stood firm. He still didn't want to do any chores, and he believed he shouldn't have to. At that point, Bernice let him have it. "What? You think you're gonna lay up in my house while everyone else is workin', readin' that trash?! What hotel do you think you're stayin' at?! You better get your skinny butt down from that bed!"

Jude must have thought he was safe from the full force of

Neecy's wrath as long as he stayed in the top bunk. That might have been true if he hadn't been leaning on the bed guard rail. Bernice grabbed a handful of pajama top and yanked Jude out in one clean-and-jerk motion. By the time his feet hit the floor, Clovis had unbuckled his belt and followed through on a beautiful forehand swing that caught Jude right on the butt-cheeks. He started to do the whuppin' dance around the room while Visey, Sammy, and I enjoyed the show. Daddy caught Jude on his leg, which only made him dance faster. Sammy whispered, "I shoulda made some popcorn."

Momma and Jude had a classic call-and-response going. Daddy made the belt snap on the verb.

"Are you gonna <u>make</u> your bed?" "Yes!"

"Are you gonna <u>clean</u> your room?" "Yes!"

"Are you gonna <u>take</u> out the garbage?" "Yes!"

By the time she was finished, Jude had committed to cleaning the entire house by himself for the next four Saturdays.

Chores changed with every house, but not the need, or the reason. Chores kept the home running and kept things from falling apart. Jude never did grow to like them, but he got very good at doing them right the first time so he could spend as little time as possible doing them. I'm not sure he learned that particular lesson on that Saturday, but I know the question of doing chores or not doing chores never came up again. I always found it ironic Jude rose to be a Chief Petty Officer in the United States Navy where the efficient running of a naval vessel was his responsibility; assigning seamen various duties. I have used the idea of chores in my own family, and my wife and I have run into the same resistance to the concept from our three kids.

TOYS MY FATHER GAVE ME

MOMMA AND DADDY had to do something to keep us occupied and entertained. They had four smart, rambunctious, rebellious boys, and keeping us busy was a full-time job. So as far back as I can remember, we were always into stuff where we could use our hands. As an electrical engineer, Daddy had soldering irons and circuit boards and vacuum tubes around all the time. He had Sammy, Jude, and Visey build a Heathkit radio and taught them radio transmission and reception.

Our basement probably could have given the Sears Toy Department a run for their money. Miraculously, four lower-middle-class boys were

Clovis kept us busy with toys that taught.

in full immersion with Lincoln Logs; Richter's Anchor Stone Building Blocks; a Lionel Model Railroad set; more than one Gilbert Chemistry Set; and, a Code Key Morse Telegraph kit. We built working microscopes, full-on Gilbert erector sets, and even the Visible Man and Visible Woman plastic models showing every detail of the human anatomy.

Clo was a very good chess player, so learning to play serious chess was a given. It was not enough to know the pieces and how they moved; you had to appreciate strategy. And not only strategy on the chess board, but how it applied to everything. Until I could predict the moves of opponents, I was at a distinct disadvantage in anything competitive. I couldn't take refuge by playing Checkers. Only sissies played checkers in our house. Mastery of Parcheesi, Monopoly, and Risk was required because much smack was talked among the Bordeaux boys, beginning with unfolding the game-board. Monopoly was a contact sport, and we played with a passion. Brotherly and familial love didn't play into anything. Momma would not participate in any of these antics; not because she couldn't compete, but because she felt angst for whichever of her sons was on the short end of the stick.

Birthdays and Christmas guaranteed receiving a puzzle of some kind from someone in our family. Not a jig-saw or anything like that. Our puzzles were those wooden cubes or balls where the pieces could only be removed or re-assembled in a certain sequence. Once, Uncle Austin gave us a wooden elephant puzzle that, because of its asymmetrical shape, should have been tough to put back together. Jude had it solved before we got home from Christmas dinner.

Daddy gave us yo-yo's and wooden tops and taught us how to use them competitively. Who knew you could split the other guy's spinning top if you "nailed" it just so with your own top? We all got pretty good with different Duncan Yo-Yo tricks. But we also had prisms and kaleidoscopes to play with light and color and gyroscopes to play with balance and motion. And at every turn, Clo would ask and explain, ask and explain.

Momma tried bravely to give us some fine arts culture. She always had sculpting clay and tempura paints around. She enrolled all of us in piano lessons, although they only stuck with Visey. When he sat down at the piano, he met his muse. When I sat down, all I met was misery. Next, she turned me to the violin. Poor Mr. Graham watched me struggle with that violin under my neck trying to position my thumb and fingers around its neck. It probably would have helped if I had practiced my scales and the like, but I didn't. I know now that Momma was paying good money for those lessons, but I wasn't thinking about that back then.

When we went out as a family, Momma and Daddy would take us to places like the Forest Preserves of Cook County, the Adler Planetarium, and The Museum of Science & Industry. Our parents were all about exposure. They were going to expose my three brothers and me to every learning opportunity they could devise. Any example or illustration of the natural world and our interaction with it would ignite Momma's elementary teacher instincts and Daddy's analytical engineering mind. We could find tools like hammers and pliers and screwdrivers and shovels to get into various kinds of mischief. Even chores became time and motion studies. Momma would engage us in some activity while Daddy would ask and explain. Planets, tree rings, El trains or atoms; she could make a question and answer game of it and he always had a question and an explanation.

When it came to toys, Momma deferred almost completely

to Daddy, and Clo was all about us being deep into 1950s popular hobbies or "project-based learning." For the Bordeaux boys that meant building models of almost anything you could get: planes, cars, and boats—even sailboats and aircraft carriers. Clo let us choose our own; we all started with planes—obviously, World War II types—like the P-47s and P51s Daddy worked on with the 332nd.

He would explain the function of each part as we assembled. We meticulously glued, painted, and displayed with pride, because Daddy would only let us move to the next phase when we had properly finished the current one. Sammy and Visey stayed with planes while Jude moved on to ships—mostly battleships and cruisers. I did cars. In addition to the muscle-car models, I built all the Chuck Barris fantasy cars from the BatMobile to the hearselike car used in the Munster's TV series. James Bond's Aston Martin with all of the operable special effects like an ejector-seat was my masterpiece. Collectively, we built a fire-engine red 1/8 scale Jaguar XKE. The doors opened, the wheels turned, and the steering worked. Magnificent!

At one point, Daddy wasn't satisfied with us just putting together models. He wanted us to fly something we'd built— a balsa-wood plane with a gas engine. Once the decision was made, he painstakingly lead us through cutting each strut and aileron from the balsa and sanding the pieces to perfection. Guide-wires, fuel lines, and a fuel tank had to be built into the wings and fuselage. The wings and fuselage were covered in paper and extremely fragile even after a couple of coats of paint. The engine had to sit just right into the nose of the plane. After a lot of work, this aeronautical miracle, painted a fire-engine red, was ready to fly! This exacting, preparatory process took FOREVER! Although I was little more than an observer, being so young, by the time we got to flight day we were all bouncing around like pinballs.

We loaded ourselves, and everything we'd need into the back of the car and Daddy drove to the football field at the high school. Clo walked out to the middle of the field and set the plane on the 50-yard line. We crowded around him as he put the gas in the tank, all the while telling us that this engine was dangerous and nothing to mess with. He sternly told Visey to gently hold the fuselage until he got Daddy's signal.

Daddy told everyone else to step back a little while he hooked the metal loop around the propeller and began cocking the prop and letting it go until the engine started. We were all duly impressed when we saw how fast the propeller was spinning but, that just boosted our excitement about getting this bad boy up in the air.

As was his custom, Daddy would demonstrate before giving one of us the reins. He would fly the plane first, so he could show us proper operation and control. I was too little to fly it, so I was already past silly and closing in on goofy. Jude kept telling me to calm down, but I was a lost cause.

After he had filled the tank and started the engine, Daddy walked the ten yards or so down the guideline to the control handle. He gripped it in his right hand and gave Visey the nod to let go of the plane. It started taxiing in a circle with Daddy as the center point and the guide wires as the radius.

The plane slowly lifted off the ground and tentatively climbed. Because the plane was tethered to Daddy, all it could do is fly in that circle. At first, its flight was uneven and erratic, but by the second or third lap, Clo had straightened that plane up and was flyin' right. Daddy kept that bird up in the air for a long while, until we started hearing the sputtering engine as it ran of gas. We all thought that a crash landing was imminent and all of our hard work was about to go up in flames like the Hindenburg. But Daddy flicked his wrist a couple of times to adjust his flaps and rudders and started to descend. When the engine ran out of gas and stopped, instead of watching a disaster, we saw Daddy land that plane perfectly and bring it to a smooth, rolling stop. My brothers and I busted into cheers for the best pilot ever. Simultaneously, we all realized that we would make a few more trips out to the football field before any of us would have the knowledge—or the nerve—to fly like Clo.

Comic Books

WE ALL KNEW where we had to be that Friday afternoon; I was in Miz Gaylor's fifth-grade class at St. Leo's while Visey was in the seventh grade. Jude and Sammy were sophomores in what would become Verbum Dei boy's Catholic high school. Construction on the new building on Central Avenue had not yet been completed, so classes were being held in the multi-purpose room at St. Leo's. In any event, my three brothers and I knew to be at the car, ready to leave immediately after the 3:00 bell rang to dismiss the Catholic school at St. Leo's parish.

The ride down Central Avenue was made in almost complete silence. There was nothing on the AM dial that Momma wanted to listen to, least of all KGFJ. We all knew she was in no mood after a long week of herding rowdy third graders. And Friday was payday; Momma was on a mission. Although the bank was open till six o'clock, everybody and their brother was going to be in line on payday Friday. The sooner she got there and got in, the sooner she could get on with her other to-do's. She had to get something for dinner, and she had to go to the drug store.

When Momma pulled the car into the parking lot, Sammy, Jude, and Visey tumbled out and started walking to our house right around the corner, but Momma kept me with her. This meant I stayed in the car while Momma went into the bank. I didn't mind that too much 'cause this shopping center had the grocery store and our drug store all in one place, so at least we didn't have to drive anywhere else. The high point would be when Momma went to get her medicine at the pharmacy; I would make a beeline for the magazine rack and all the new comic books.

I got lost in my normal daydreaming, and it seemed like Momma came out of the bank almost as soon as she went in. I rolled up the windows, locked the car, and ran to catch up to Momma just as she went into the grocery store. We both knew what we were there to get. It was Friday, and we were Catholic. We made our way to the pasta aisle and got the makings for spaghetti. We cruised to the frozen food aisle and found the breaded shrimp and cheese pizza the four Bordeaux boys loved. This was a serious treat 'cause everybody loved fried shrimp. Daddy would have to police the allocation of shrimp at the dinner table to make sure everyone got three shrimp each. We tolerated the pizza 'cause we all thought pizza without sausage was sacrilege. Finally, Momma grabbed a head of lettuce and a tomato for Clo's salad. The last things to go in the cart were two big bottles of Shasta soda: root beer for us and cream soda for Momma and Daddy. When we got outside, I took Momma's keys and struggled to carry the paper grocery bags to the car. Meanwhile, she walked over to the drug store. I ran to catch up, and we made it to the automatic door at almost the same time.

I loved the drug store. A sanitized, instrumental version of "Girl from Ipanema" was playing on the loudspeaker. The vacuum-tube testing booth stood to the right. I had accompanied Daddy on many a visit to that booth as he kept his early, high fidelity sound equipment, television and radios working with this convenient testing booth and I had a ball twisting and turning the various knobs and dials. There was a toy section with toy cars and water guns. The ice cream counter always had customers; I figured because the ice cream 'scoops' came out as cylinders rather than spheres so you got more for your fifteen cents. Momma went toward the pharmacy area, and I sped to the magazine rack, bypassing the daily newspapers, Time, Life, Look, and the Saturday Evening Post. My objective was comic books.

At that time, I was a DC-comics geek; Superman, Batman, the Flash, Green Lantern—I knew them all. Of course, I was following in my brothers' footsteps. These were the comics they read, so they were handed down, and I read them too—if I wanted to. But MAD magazine was "required" reading among the Bordeaux boys. I can trace my warped sense of humor and appreciation of the absurd to reading MAD and other satire magazines. There were public figures, issues, and events that I first encountered in the pages of MAD Magazine. There were regular features like 'SPY vs. SPY' that consistently illustrated the absurdity of one-ups-man-ship. Jude and Sammy used to argue about who got to do the fold-y picture in the inside back cover.

Momma hated comic books. She made a show of voicing her distaste for comic books of all stripes. As far as she was concerned, they were a waste of money, paper, time, and talent—and had absolutely no redeeming social value. And then MAD Magazine? Why did this goofy Alfred E. Newman, staring out from the cover of every issue, merit our allegiance?

Nevertheless, we read every comic book (and MAD issue) we could get our hands on. There was this open conspiracy of us defying the rule of Momma, and never really suffering any consequences. She didn't take the comics away, but she let us know at every turn how she felt about them.

So there I was standing by the magazine rack, staring at the brand new MAD. Neither Sammy nor Jude had this issue. I would be the baddest Bordeaux boy if I came home with it! I would even get to be the first to do the fold-y thing, which looked like it might be good this time. But there was a problem; I had no money. With my meager allowance, I couldn't afford the dime for the DC comic books, so I knew MAD would be out of my reach. Maybe Momma would buy it for me? I dismissed that as stupid as fast I thought of it.

I picked it up and riffed through the pages, recognizing all of the regular features like 'A MAD Look at…', 'Don Martin Gags,' and 'the Lighter Side of…' which all skewered the prevailing norms of the day. That's when it happened. The thought and the act of cramming the magazine down my pants occurred almost simultaneously. I didn't have time to adjust things and started moving very carefully toward the checkout. Momma turned the corner from the pharmacy and walked past me to the waiting clerk. I got up close to her as she paid for her medicine and suddenly stopped cold. For some reason, my behavior caught Momma's attention, and she turned to me. At that very moment, the magazine slid down my leg and exited near my left shoe. The look of mortification on her face hit me right between my eyes. She scrambled to dig out some change and paid for the magazine. She grabbed up her bags with one hand and me with the other—her grip on my wrist like a vice. I was dragged so forcefully I didn't feel my feet on the ground until we were at the car. She couldn't find the keys, of course, because I had them. As I handed them over, feeling worse by the minute, she said in an eerily calm voice, "We are going to talk about this when we get home. Get in the car."

I sat next to her in the front seat wishing we had a long drive ahead of us. I knew what Momma called "talking about," I called "a whuppin'." I figured as soon as the car stopped in our driveway, the whuppin' would commence. It took all of three minutes to drive around the corner. When she stopped the car, I jumped out and went straight to my room. Momma was in hot pursuit and was there before I could climb in the top bunk. Sammy, Jude, and Visey saw all this, and they knew something was afoot. Momma slammed the door in their faces and then turned to me.

"YOU STOLE A COMIC BOOK. I HAVE TO GO IN THAT STORE EVERY WEEK AND NOW I'M THE WOMAN WHOSE SON STEALS COMIC BOOKS!" She stared at me, wheezing with anger. "What do you have to say for yourself?" I started to say something; she screamed, "SHUT UP WHEN I'M TALKING TO YOU!"

Bernice was not a big woman, but she was towering over me like a linebacker. She asked me why I had to steal that trash and why I couldn't just save my money and buy it if I wanted it that bad? I had no answers to this or the questions that followed. I was reeling from everything when she reached up and snatched a rubber-tipped bamboo spear Visey had gotten at Knott's Berry Farm and swung on my butt in one smooth motion. She was reaching back for a second swing before I even realized the whuppin' had commenced. I could hear my brothers cracking up every time I yelled out. Momma wasn't hitting me very hard, but a whuppin' with a bamboo spear hurt under any circumstances. All of a sudden, she stopped swinging. She was wheezing and sweating and still mad. She said quietly, "I am going to tell your father, and you will have to square this with him."

I mumbled, "Yes'm."

"Where is the comic book?" I did not know. I hadn't seen it since it fell out of my pants. She reached for the purse she dropped when she came in my room and threw the offending magazine at me, pages flailing open. It hit me in the chest and fell in my lap. She told me to start tearing. I tried, but I couldn't—until I realized I would have to tear the pages out one at a time until the whole thing was scraps on the floor. My tears were soaking the paper when Momma said calmly, "If you want to act like a thief, we are going to treat you like a thief. If you want to be a member of this family, you are going to have to fix this. Tomorrow, you are going to walk into that store and apologize to the manager for your behavior. Do you understand?" I did understand, but on that day, I did not know how I could ever undo the look of disappointment in my mother's eyes. I was still susceptible to 'the look.' My parent's disapproval mattered to me-and my mother's mattered most of all-even if it mattered less and less to each of my brothers.

For the longest time, I suspected that this episode was the first thing my mother thought of when she saw me. You couldn't tell me otherwise, but this was not the case. Momma had much more important things on her mind. Her health; her other sons; her job. Nevertheless I kept trying to meet her expectations of me: grades, general behavior around the house, doing the inevitable chores, helping her through her increasingly frequent asthma attacks. I found this was a really good way to keep Momma and Daddy happy and for me to earn the kind of independence I wanted. I also learned the value of something stolen or unearned is hollow and illusory. Earned achievement and accomplishment is robust and lasting.

The King's English

DADDY LOVED THE "King's English" and used it well. Nothing drove him farther around the bend than the misuse of the English language by a speaker who didn't know better. And Momma, being a teacher, was even harder on folks' proper use of English than Daddy. Now I don't want to suggest that my parents cared more about diction and pronunciation than communication. Rather, they were absolutely determined to make sure their sons could use the language. They appreciated accents, dialects, colloquialisms and even the odd instance of slang. But still, they fervently believed that knowledge of proper English was the necessary foundation for successful communication. Momma, however, was our Grammar Cop. She was just this side of annoying with her corrections, but we took her instruction without comment. To complain about being reminded not to drop a 'g' was to invite Momma's middle-finger pop to the back of your head. She held herself and Daddy to the same standard. The only time Momma would slip up and speak without perfect grammar and diction was when she was "half-past mad." Of course, raising four Bordeaux boys would be enough to put any mother to the test, so our household did hear its fair share of common vernacular from Bernice. But when she was all the way past mad, what I would call "beyond" anger, she spoke slowly and correctly, like the teacher she was. She would say things like, "Lord, have mercy." With an exasperated sigh. It was like standing inside the eye-wall of a hurricane—calm and orderly. But we knew that when she cut loose and said, "You must have lost your mind!" havoc would ensue.

Both our parents would cringe every time a Black "Anybody" was interviewed and mangled the language. To their minds, mastering English was a prerequisite to having a microphone in your face, and any inarticulateness, especially the misuse of a word, was a sign of ignorance and an embarrassment to the rest of us. Their assessment was most harsh when directed toward athletes who had been given scholarships to get an education and still sounded "uncouth."

This is why Daddy held someone like the late tennis player and social activist Arthur Ashe in such high esteem. First of all, Daddy played tennis for at least seventy-five years! He and his best friend Rob Taylor learned the game from the man who would go on to discover and coach Ashe through his youth career up to his years at UCLA—Dr. Walter Johnson.

Remember, now, before Arthur Ashe, the only black face seen on the Grand Slam tennis circuit was Althea Gibson (also coached by Johnson) on the women's side. When Ashe came along and competed at the highest levels as an amateur, his ability to focus and remain unperturbed by hostile surroundings gave Daddy an overwhelming sense of pride. Part of this pride was Daddy's respect for someone being "a first." He and Ashe shared knowledge of the difficulties, challenges and daily indignities Ashe (and others) had endured and overcome. Admittedly, part of Daddy's pride developed in reaction to the loud and crass players like Nastase and Connors. Ashe rose above all of that. And then, when Ashe spoke, it was with clarity, wit and a deadpan humility that reflected intelligence and thoughtfulness. As Daddy said a million times, "This cat was SMOOTH!"

What Daddy valued about the language above all else was precision. He used his words to say what he meant. He enjoyed applying ridiculously precise margins of error to everyday stuff (facetiously, he would say each of his beloved green grapes had to be the same size +/- 5 micrograms). Love of language and detail was not unique to him; it was part of the Bordeaux Family. Clo's brothers and sisters all shared it to one extent or another. His mother and all his siblings spoke with brevity and clarity. Whenever two or more of them got together, their love of language, combined with a droll, dry, ironic sense of humor, served to pepper their conversation on topics from sports to politics and civil rights. Their knowledge of the language included clever wordplay and (awful!) puns. And they could slip into 1940's slang and cool vernacular for effect or to make a point. As a lifelong reader, Clo would consume everything from dime-store pulp novels to the Scientific American journals that were always near his favorite recliner. References from his reading would inform and populate his conversations.

It all came from Daddy's mother, Elizabeth. She had trained to be a teacher. In those days, this meant getting a two-year "normal school" teaching certificate. When her husband Sam died, she went to the St. Louis Board of Education to apply for a teaching job. The Superintendent at the time denied her application because married women could not teach in the schools. Elizabeth pointed out that she was not married; she was a widow. A distinction without a difference. The superintendent would not relent. Middle of the Depression. Seven children—seven mouths to feed. No job. Grandma Elizabeth ended up washing and folding sheets at Homer G. Phillips Hospital. Her three girls; Dominca, Elizabeth and Olive, would be sent to live for a time in an orphanage.

Still, she did not let her training go to waste. She collaborated with her kids' teachers to know what was going on in the classroom. She applied the appropriate corrective measures when someone's performance was not up to snuff. Although Daddy describes himself as a so-so student, he knew better than to tangle with his mother. He studied enough to get the grades he needed to keep her happy. It wasn't until he graduated from Sumner High School and followed his buddy, Rob, to Lincoln University that he found out what a good student he was. There he discovered he had learned through osmosis, and retained, a lot more knowledge in high school than he thought. In the process, he charted a path for his brothers and sister to pursue higher education. Donald and Liz also went to Lincoln. Austin would later go to Cal State LA and USC. A love of learning and the King's English is a cornerstone of our family. We are and always have been a family that believed in education. Three of the four of us Bordeaux boys got college degrees. Most of our children have pursued higher education, and that legacy continues through the generations. We have also learned and appreciated and practiced the best use of English in our lives and careers. And even, if not especially, through difficult times, this family habit of speaking the King's English has served us well.

BIKES

BACK IN THE day, the ability to fix a bike was an absolute survival skill in our family. Does your seat need adjusting? Get a wrench and adjust it. Flat tire? Find out why and fix it. Handlebars, chains, tires, brakes, et al., were the do-it-yourself domain of the Bordeaux boys. Ergo, if I wanted to roll with my brothers or my friends, I had to learn to fix and to care for my bike. It had to be ready for whatever I wanted to do, for wherever and whenever I wanted to go.

Our dedication to well maintained bikes started back in Chicago. Daddy wanted to give each of his boys a bike, but the cost of bikes for four boys was prohibitive. That's when he saw an ad in the Sun-Times for the police auction. This was a regularly scheduled sale of seized or recovered-but-unclaimed property. Clo bid on and bought four bikes, all in pretty good condition, for the cost of only one bike from Sears or Monkey Wards (the moniker many used for Montgomery Wards). They had been sitting in the Police Impound for an unknown length of time and were dusty and rusty. But Daddy had a plan.

When Clo parked the black Ford Country Squire station wagon behind the house, we were unprepared for the surprise he would pull out of the back. Sammy, Jude, Visey, and I tumbled outside and across the yard to the back gate. I brought up the rear because I was always last, and neither Visey nor I understood what was happening. Momma just watched from the kitchen 'cause she wasn't about to get in the way of the pre-teen tidal wave that was overtaking Daddy. As he opened the back gate of the car, we still didn't recognize the tangle of metal, rubber, and plastic. It wasn't until he pulled Sammy's bike out of the car that Visey and I got it. That bike was a chrome boy's Schwinn with fenders over two flat tires and a red seat. It was gorgeous! Sammy was instantly in love, and Jude was instantly jealous—until he saw the second bike. It was also a Schwinn boy's, but this one was dark blue, no fenders, and the handlebars drooped from being stripped.

Visey's bike was red, the next size down from Sammy and Jude's. His tires were not only flat but dry and cracked. And it didn't have a seat. I almost passed out from the excitement of seeing my brothers go crazy over their new rides. I knew mine would round out the quartet. In my mind's eye, I could see us riding down the street, four-abreast, as we were checked out and cheered by fellow bike riders from all over the neighborhood. That's when I saw mine. I was all of seven years old and could barely ride without training wheels. What was a completely appropriate size bicycle for me, and one Daddy was right to snag, was disappointing. When I saw the small, dull black, nondescript bike next to the blue and red and chrome pedal rockets of my brothers, I was crushed. Well, that childhood appraisal was about to change.

Daddy wrestled the four bikes down into the basement and set them in an arc around the workbench where he kept his tools. Two of the bikes had kick-stands, so he grabbed one and yanked on the handlebars as the bike rolled forward. He flipped the bike over and balanced it in a three-point stance on the seat and handlebars. We raced to mimic this and flipped the remaining bikes. Daddy grabbed my hands on my handlebars and flipped the little bike with me. Jude's bike with the droopy handlebars wouldn't balance until Clo tightened the nut as much as he could. Visey's bike didn't have a seat, so Daddy strategically placed a couple of blocks of wood to support his bike's weight. Once we had the bikes flipped, we waited for the next thing Daddy would do.

He started at the front of Sammy's bike. He looked at the tires for wear and punctures. We quickly started looking at our tires. Jude, with his two flat and cracked tires, wandered over to Sammy's bike. Visey and I didn't know what we were looking at or for, but we made a big show of spinning the wheel and inspecting the tire. We got sidetracked when I started spinning my tire as fast as I could. I was in my own little world until I noticed it was quiet and looked up. Daddy and my brothers were looking at me like I had lost my mind. As soon as they realized that I realized they were staring at me, we all broke into snickers and giggles and then outright laughing. We were bustin' up so much that Momma ran down the basement stairs to see what was going on. When Daddy told her what happened, she started laughing along with everybody else. I was laughing the hardest even though I don't think I knew what was so funny. But it was one of those Bordeaux family moments that you don't forget for a long time. A lifetime.

We got back to the task at hand. Daddy looked over our shoulders at each of the bikes and made a note of which tires he would replace in addition to the seat and handlebars he already knew he needed. He then took a wrench and a pair of pliers off the workbench and gave a try at loosening the nuts on the front wheel of Sammy's bike. When the nuts wouldn't give, Daddy got a tall, slender, red-and-black-and-white can of 3-IN-1 Oil. As he squeezed the oil out of the can, there was a hollow knock with every squeeze—the sound of air getting in the can. He put a couple of drops on the nut on the left side and gave the can to Sammy to oil the nut on the right side. Sammy grabbed the can with both hands and was about to spray oil on the nut, the axle, and half the spokes, until Daddy stopped him with a firm, "Gently." That way of correcting his sons, of "teaching" us was a characteristic of Daddy that never changed. I think about it every time I'm in a position to advise or mentor someone coming behind me. He would reach back and give back at every turn: community activist, mentor, tutor. Like Clovis, I've tried to pass along my meager wisdom to any young person who asks for my help.

Daddy turned to Jude's bike and repeated the process. The nuts gave on the first tug, but he had Jude squirt some oil on the nuts anyway. He was careful to point to where the oil was supposed to go. Daddy asked Sammy to find some rags and told Jude to go upstairs, put the stopper in the tub and run the water for a couple of minutes. He moved on to Visey's and my bikes and watched us as we glopped the oil on the nuts and everything else. Sammy returned with some old shirt remnants just in time. Daddy called up to Jude and told him to turn off the water.

Once we all had the nuts on the front wheels loosened, Daddy took the wheels off Visey's bike and then helped each of us follow suit. Sammy's bike had a front fender, so we all got to see how the fender attached to the axle. Daddy took a screwdriver and cautiously pried the flat tire away from the wheel's rim. When he could, he pulled the tire away from the rim with his fingers. We were all going crazy 'cause Daddy was so adept and sure about what he was doing, and we wanted to do that to our wheels. We didn't know it then, but Daddy was instilling in us patience that would serve us in every aspect of our lives. At that time, we just wanted to get everything done now!

He showed us the inner tube and valve stem, and we saw him push in the valve stem through the wheel rim and yank out the inner tube from inside the tire in one clean motion. He grabbed a bicycle pump from the corner and a can of tire patches out of his toolbox. He took the inner tube and started running up the stairs, taking them two-at-a-time. Sammy told him he better not let Momma see him running like that. "She'll give you something to run from," he said in his best Momma-impersonation voice.

When Daddy got to the bathroom, he screwed the pump to the valve stem and got to pumpin.' We could see the inner tube inflate, and Jude and Sammy both wanted to pump. Daddy stopped the argument by telling us there were eight tires downstairs. Everybody was gonna get a chance to pump. He gave the pump five more good strokes and deftly unscrewed the pump from the valve. He then threw the tube in the tub and did his best to hold it underwater.

Clo started with the valve stem and examined it with his engineer's eye. "I'm looking for leaks," he said to no one in particular. We were all shoving and craning our necks to see what he was doing. When no leaks were found around the stem, he moved clockwise around the inner tube. Everybody but me saw whatever happened next because in his excitement to watch Daddy, Sammy's elbow caught me right across the nose. No harm, no foul, but while everyone else was ooh-in' and ahh-in' around Daddy, I was seeing stars.

Consequently, I was clueless as to what was going on. Sammy saw that I was wincing and trying to keep up with the activities. He rubbed the bridge of my nose and made a big deal out of looking in my eyes and up my nose. He asked if I was okay and I nodded. Then he pulled me in front of Jude and Visey so I could see better. Sammy could be like that.

I soon understood that the ooh-in' and ahh-in' was about a steady stream of tiny air bubbles coming out of the innertube. Clo reached for the sliver of Ivory soap near the tub with one hand and held the thumb of his other hand on the spot where the bubbles were escaping. He wiped the inner tube on his shirt and then scribbled an "X" with the soap bar to mark the spot. Daddy told Visey to take the top off the tire repair kit can, but Visey complained that the top of the can could scratch him. Daddy said, "Just be careful with it. I need it to scuff the tire up." Sammy asked what he meant. Daddy said, "It's easier to show than explain it to you." He then proceeded to flip the top of the tire repair kit can and scraped and scratched the tire right where the soapy "X" was. "You scuff up the rubber tire so the glue and the patch will stick better." We nodded in unanimous, enthusiastic, partial understanding. I understood the 'glue' and 'stick.'

Daddy laid the inner tube aside and found his hair-cutting scissors in the drawer. He emptied the tire patch can and cut an inch-square section from a larger piece. As soon as the larger piece fell in the sink, Sammy and Jude were on it, both trying to be the first to inspect it. Clo nipped that in the bud with a look. When we were all focused on him, he was rounding the corners of the small square. He took a tiny tube and unscrewed the top. He picked up the inner tube and smooshed a dab of glue right on the "X" and spread the glue around with the glue tube before blowing on it and setting it down again. He then peeled a thin piece of paper backing off the patch and settled it down in the glue smoosh. He held it in place for a minute or two until he had put his scissors and the soap away. He told Visey to put the glue and rubber patch away and put the top back on the tire patch. He grabbed a washcloth and pressed the top on so it wouldn't scratch him again.

We all trailed behind Daddy back down to the basement. He had the inner tube in one hand and the pump in the other. When we got downstairs, Daddy screwed the pump onto the stem and invited Sammy to pump. "Give it five pumps." He gave us all a chance to pump, although my five pumps added zero pounds of pressure to the equation. Daddy stopped us and inspected the inner tube. The patch was holding, and there didn't seem to be any other leaks.

We let the air out of the tire and put the inner tube back in the tire, and then all started working on our respective bikes and tires. Every time somebody got an inner tube out of a tire, we knew the drill. Over the next week, we fixed all the leaks in the inner tubes that would go into the new tires, and we fixed the seats and handlebars. Finally, my brothers and I could see our bikes assembling before our eyes. I still had a little bit of jealousy when I looked at the chrome and blue and red rides of my brothers and then at my little black bike. But as time went on, I learned how to ride on that bike. I learned the mechanics of a bike on that thing. I learned a bike is a bike is a bike. Understand one; you understand them all. We were soon riding our bikes as a matter of course, and their presence became the new normal.

At some point, another bike showed up. I don't know if it was new or a Police Auction special. What I do know is that all of a sudden Sammy was riding the new bike and Jude was riding the chrome bike. Visey was not going to be left behind, and he grabbed Jude's bigger blue bike. I was left looking at Visey's red bike and thinking it was too big for me. I musta' looked at that red bike for a week before I screwed up the courage to try and ride it. Daddy saw me sitting on it with my feet barely touching the pedals. He lowered the seat and adjusted the handlebars and all of a sudden, the red bike fit me. He called it a 'hand-me-down' bike. He could tell by the quizzical look on my face that I didn't get it. "Sammy got a new bike and handed his down to Jude. Jude handed his bike down to Visey, and Visey handed his bike down to you." This process would repeat itself again and again. I decided how that worked was pretty cool, but I never liked the hand-me-down moniker. What my three older brothers saw as handing me down their discards and don't-wants, I saw as my opportunity to get a step-up. There are some perks to being the youngest. Now that I think about it, that pre-teen insight grew into an attitude that moves me to count my blessings and look for the best in anything that comes my way, however dire they might appear. There have been instances in my life where I could not change the circumstances, but I could change the way I thought about those circumstances.

When we moved to Pomona in the summer of '64, it was at precisely the same time Schwinn introduced the Stingray; a small, mobile, stylish bike that had a bunch of distinctive characteristics. The iconic banana seat had a chrome support bar attached to the rear axle—for some reason nicknamed a "sissy bar." The butterfly handlebars were inspired by the exaggerated motorcycle handlebars of "chopper" motorcycle fame. The knobby tires hummed on the blacktop. I loved the Stingray. I coveted a Stingray. I had to have a Stingray.

Everything about the Stingray was different. The bike was purposely undersized, so you had to sit farther over the back tire. Hence the elongated banana seat. This change in the center of gravity and the butterfly handlebars also made it easier to yank the front wheel up off the ground in a "wheelie." There were guys in Pomona who could go for a city block with that wheel in the air, pedaling all the while. Me? I couldn't go from one driveway to the next—on my friends' Stingrays. There were other accessories too like chrome flared half-fenders or vinyl handlebar wraps in just about every color known to man, and new handlebar-grips to match. You could go way over the top with mirrors or lights, but I preferred just the essential bike.

I longed for a bike like that for a couple of years., I had eventually inherited Sammy's chrome bike, although the only things left of the original were the frame, sprocket, and chain. I had changed out everything on that bike, including a very cool set of butterfly handlebars. In the process, I honed my maintenance skills not only on my own but on friends' bikes for the occasional soda or ice cream sandwich.

I rode my bike everywhere. I rode to St Joseph's every day in the sixth and seventh grades. I had a Progress Bulletin paper route for a minute. I was a regular at the comic book shop and the slot car track, both on Holt, near Garey, right around the corner from the bike shop. Once, I rode all the way to the Sears mall at Indian Hill to do my Christmas shopping.

In the summer before eighth grade, I decided it was time

for me to have a Stingray. Once I made that decision, I couldn't stop thinking about the "how." Clo and Bernice were not going to pay for a bike when: a) I already had a bike; and, b) they were well aware of my bike-building prowess because I told them about it at every opportunity. I quickly concluded that if I was going to own a Stingray, I would have to build it myself. I started looking for a Stingray-like frame and thought that just a frame from a smaller bike might do. I soon discovered it would not accommodate the larger Stingray tires, and that my new bike would require a larger sprocket for the pedals. But I had already spent five dollars, and now I had nothing to show for it but a head-shake from Clo that told me I had a lot to learn about building a bike from scratch.

The trouble was that everybody wanted a Stingray, so these bicycle frames weren't just laying around. The bike shop wanted thirty dollars for a scratched-up green one, but I didn't have the money, and I hated the color green. The only other frames I came across were being sold by a real shady dude who lived over on Belinda, and I suspected they were from stolen bikes. I didn't want any part of that. I could just imagine building a bike from a stolen frame and having some kid call me out. I was even more fearful that Clovis and Bernice would discover I had trafficked in stolen goods. Momma would still be whuppin' my behind.

Even in the eighth grade, Johnny Bean was a neighborhood legend. I didn't know why, but everyone in Sintown knew about Johnny Bean. The word most often associated with Johnny was "juvie," although I couldn't tell you if he had ever spent any time there. He had a way of walking and talking and acting that made him seem grown up, even though he was our age. He was always talking to the finest girls in Sintown, and they all liked Johnny Bean.

Our garage was in front of our house at the end of a curved driveway, and when the garage door was open, you could see what was going on from the street. It was dusk on a Friday, and I was working on a bike in the garage when Johnny and a few other dudes started doo-woppin' under the street lamp. I looked out and saw a big bottle of orange soda changing hands. Then I heard a few bars of "Up On the Roof" and a string of adolescent profanities. I had never spoken to Johnny, and he had never spoken to me, but during a break in the action, Johnny walked up my driveway and asked what I was doing. I tried to explain my tinkering on bikes and how I wanted to build a Stingray, but I couldn't find a frame. I was a nerd, a geek, and a square who was just exiting Catholic school to go into public school, so I didn't know what to make of this audience with the mysterious Johnny Bean. I later found out that Johnny knew my brother, Visey, and was actually looking for him.

Anyway, Johnny asked me a couple more questions, like what color Stingray frame I was looking for and had I talked to this guy over on Farringdon or that guy who lived over there. I kinda shook my head and said, "Naw." Then suddenly, the conversation ended. Johnny went back to sippin' and singin', and I closed the garage and went into the house.

A couple of weeks later, I went out to the garage to do the regular chores I did on Saturday because there were cartoons to watch and I wanted to make a run to the comic book store. Up against the garage door was a metallic blue Stingray bike frame. It was completely stripped. It had no sprocket, chain, pedals, bearings or anything else. I was immediately exhilarated and scared to death at the same time. There was the very Stingray bike frame I had been searching for, but I had no idea how it ended up leaning against my garage. If Daddy asked me about it, I would have nothing to tell him. How was I going to explain this? Was it stolen? If it was stolen, who stole it? Who put it up against our garage? Could I keep it?

I quickly opened the garage, swooped the bike frame inside, and hid it behind a bunch of stuff. I was rationalizing my butt off, telling myself I didn't steal no bike frame. If anything, I found it, and in the time-honored playground tradition of "Finders Keepers, Losers Weepers," that bike frame was mine. It took me two days, till Clo went to work on Monday, to pull that frame out and look it over. I slipped one of my tires in the rear of the frame, and it fit like a dream. I decided not to look a gift horse in the mouth and started tinkering. I soon realized that I already had some of the parts I would need, but once I started building my dream StringRay, I would be without a bike because I was going to have to cannibalize my big chrome bike for those parts. The rest I would have to buy or get in trade. But I got to work anyway.

I started with the simple stuff, like the butterfly handlebars. They came off Big Chrome and went onto the Stingray. I had gotten a hold of the rims and tires a while ago, so they went on next, although it would soon seem like I put those tires on and took them off five times a day until the bike was completed. A fellow bike nerd upgraded his banana seat to a nice metal-flake, candy-apple-red one and sold me his old, black faux tuck-'n-roll for three dollars. He threw in the sissy bar for two dollars. I figured I was only a few days from a completed Stingray, and I could already see myself cruising through Sintown, barely acknowledging my multitude of admirers.

Let's just say I was mistaken. Between running out of

money buying parts and scraping almost all of my knuckles, it would be almost a month before I would be ready to ride. A big part of the delay in completing the bike was that I was not going to ask my dad for help even though I knew he could answer any question I asked. And luckily, Clo never really asked me about the bike frame—I think because he and his brothers had built and repaired their share of bikes in his day and probably worked on a few of questionable provenance. He wouldn't have taken over the assembly, but he would have silently reviewed everything I had assembled and mentally given me a 'grade.' I wasn't ready for that yet. I wanted him to assess the whole bike; once I was done building it. This meant a lot of trial and error—a lot of putting together and taking apart stuff. A lot of feeling like a doofus when something finally worked after five tries. But by the time I was finished, I knew that Stingray inside and out and I was ready to ride.

When I had first 'found' the Stingray frame, I had bought some metallic blue handlebar wrap and grips to match. One Friday evening in August, I was out in the garage tinkering; making sure the bike was mechanically ready. I could finally start dressing the bike to my tastes. I polished all the greasy fingerprints off the frame and rims. I wiped some stuff on the tires to make them shine. I pumped the tires precisely to the recommended pressure. I adjusted the butterfly handlebars ten times, so they sat at just the right angle. I was kneeling next to the bike, looking through the frame, when I saw Johnny Bean walking down Avalon with two other brothers. For some reason, my mind immediately connected Johnny and the bicycle frame. I had no proof that he had left it at my garage door, and I certainly wasn't going to ask him about it. I guess I figured that if he knew anything about it, he would tell me. I got very uncomfortable as I saw him break off from his friends and walk up the driveway.

Johnny came in the garage with that slow stroll of his and asked me what was up, and I mumbled some kind of response, "Nothin'. I'm just about finished with this bike." "I see," he said. Johnny Bean always looked and sounded like he was getting ready to bust up, so you never knew if he was serious or not. He asked me if he could sit on the bike and I told him to go ahead. He was tall and angular, and his body hung in a perpetually cool slouch. This was never more so than when he sat on my Stingray. I immediately realized that he looked cooler on that bike than I ever would. His left leg was a natural kickstand, and his right arm kinda draped off the handlebar. At first, I didn't hear the question.

"You mind if I borrow your bike?"

When I finally heard it, I was stunned. Johnny Bean wanted to borrow my bike! My hand-made Stingray! "Sure!" I said, enthusiastically surrendering the bike I had just labored over and on which I had spent the last two months' allowance. As Bugs Bunny used to say, "What a maroon." (It was his way of saying "Moron" about Elmer Fudd.)

Johnny turned the butterfly handlebars expertly and swooped out of the driveway in one easy motion. You could tell the seat and handlebars were adjusted for a smaller person, but Johnny didn't seem to mind. As soon as I saw him turn the corner toward Five-Points, I realized I hadn't asked him where he was going, or for how long. I told myself he was just riding up to Alpha Beta and would be right back. I stayed out in the garage until after ten o'clock waiting for my bike to come home. When I got up the next morning and looked around outside the garage twice, I started to get scared. How was I going to explain lending my bike to a guy like Johnny to Clo and Bernice? I started to wonder if I was ever going to see my Stingray again; and if I did, what condition was it going to be in? I visualized Johnny careening down the back roads of Ganesha Hills on my brand-new bike before I had a chance to do it myself. He was probably talking to one of the many fine sisters in Sintown ON MY BIKE!

I stayed around the house all that Saturday waiting on my bike. I washed and vacuumed both cars. I even cut the grass and trimmed the ivy plants in front of the house so I could be there when my bike came home. The longer I waited, the madder I got. Finally, around eight o'clock at night, Johnny comes rolling up the driveway. Before I could say anything, he started telling me how he had meant to bring the bike right back to me, but as soon as he reached home, his Auntie had taken him to L.A., and he just got back. He told me the bike had been locked in his garage the whole time. The Stingray was exactly as I had loaned it to him—no worse for wear. He parked it and thanked me again. Then he ran off with this loping gait that took him halfway down the block in only a few strides.

I went back in the garage and gave the bike a real close look-over. It was fine. I began thinking about the origins of my Stingray and the mysterious appearance of a bicycle frame in just the color I wanted. Did Johnny Bean have anything to do with that? I don't know, but I saw the look on his face when he sat on that bike like he was seeing an old friend. I wondered if he was telling the truth about where the bike had been, but then again, I had no reason to doubt him. Johnny and I never discussed the bike, and he never asked to borrow it again. But to this day, I think of that Stingray being as much Johnny's as mine.

SINTOWN

WE LIVED ON the west end of Pomona, the first part of town you see as you head east on the 10 Freeway just after coming over the Covina Hills near Cal Poly. The Bordeaux family was part of the great migration of black folks from the South and Midwest in the 50s and 60s. We had moved from Chicago a few years before, and now we had moved again

The Bordeaux's, circa 1965.

from Compton to Pomona. Bernice and Clovis—Neecy and Clo to friends and relatives—were Momma and Daddy to us. My brothers, Sammy, Jude, and Visey were six, five, and four years older than me respectively.

In the days before the 60, 57, and 210 freeways; the 10 was the only way into and out of the Pomona Valley—except for the 71 that took you down to the 55 and the beach. The first time Daddy drove us out to Pomona from Compton, Sammy and Jude argued about Garvey Avenue in Covina versus Garey Avenue in Pomona. Visey incessantly asked questions about where we were going to go to school. I just stared out the window as the landscape got browner and more dull.

We noticed that it was hot out here. We could even see the grey-brown smog that hung in the air of the Pomona Valley. More importantly, the further east we went, the harder it was to hear our favorite stations on the radio. Staions like KGFJ played all the Motown and Stax hits and kept my brothers tappin' and snappin' in the back seat. AM radio was all we cared about because, in 1964, we were still a few years away from the FM explosion of jazz on KBCA-105 and rock n' roll on KLOS and KMET. Our car didn't have an FM receiver anyway, so AM was all we knew. Stations with stronger signals were a good back-up and lasted all the way home, but nobody in the car was interested in the Beatles, Beach Boys, Stones, or anything like that. Tuning to one of those Top 40 stations was like admitting defeat. One station had Wolfman Jack, but Momma wasn't having any part of that.

We knew when we hit the shopping center in Covina; the signal would start fading. As the youngest Bordeaux, I sat in the front with Momma and Daddy, so I learned to tune the radio with the delicate touch of a surgeon. I could bleed the last bit of signal from it, especially if there were a song playing like Little Anthony and the Imperials', "I Think I'm Goin' Out of My Head" or Smokey singing, "Tracks of My Tears." Leaving the reach of our favorite radio stations was a metaphor for leaving the city—leaving the sounds of Black south Los Angeles where we knew the mortuaries, churches, and businesses advertised on our stations. We had always been a city family-first in Chicago and then Los Angeles. Now, we were headed for the suburbs and losing our tunes. It felt like we were losing a friend.

You could see Ganesha High School from the 10 freeway. We lived on Avalon, the first right off Ganesha Boulevard, just past the high school. All the adults referred to the tract of homes we lived in as "Valwood II." "Valwood I" was the next tract over and the houses looked a little bigger, but were probably churned out in the same post-war boom that created the rest of suburban Los Angeles. It is imperative to understand that the name "Valwood" was a creation of some real estate developer. The real, true, undisputed, and incontrovertible name of our neighborhood was SINTOWN.

Don't ask me where the name came from or what it means. I've been told an urban myth that it was named for the houses that were used for the activities of some wife-swapping employees from the old General Dynamics plant. Daddy hated the name and petitioned for some kind of redress, but to no avail. As a tax-paying adult worried about property values, I now understand how he felt. Sintown sounds awful, but it was the hood for a bunch of fine people who didn't take it too seriously. Sintown produced teachers, lawyers, scientists, military men and women, writers, politicians, a world-heavyweight champion, a few other professional athletes, and a couple of generations of people who know the truth: There were the Islands on the north side and the Village on the south side. And then there was Sintown.

Avalon was the main entry point to Sintown, but you could drive in and out on the back-side from Augusta or Academy.

It only had ten streets, so it was hard to get lost. Often, directions to somebody's crib were given in relation to someone else's house. "You know where Chuckie lives? Well, so-and-so lives right across the street."

If there was a main drag in Sintown, it was Belinda Avenue. It just seemed that everyone who was anyone lived on Belinda. I always thought of it as the capital of Sintown. Although the elementary school that served the youngest kids was a few blocks away, Marshall Jr. High and Ganesha High were easy walking distance, even from the heart of the tract. This was especially true for kids who came through the Hole in the Fence, our official backside entry and exit point to the school grounds. Sintown wrapped around the high school like a catcher's mitt, so if your street emptied onto Cromwell, you went through the Hole in the Fence at some point to get on to Ganesha's campus. When we moved to Pomona in 1964, we were one of the first Black families to do so. By the time I entered high school four years later, our neighborhood was ninety percent Black, as a result, during the 60s and early 70s, Ganesha's Black population was a pretty good reflection of our Sintown neighborhood. There were students whose parents had moved out of South Central Los Angeles alongside students from families who migrated from places like Norfolk, Virginia and Baton Rouge, Louisiana. And there were kids from military families who left to another stationing as suddenly as they arrived.

But whatever our origin points, African American families migrating to places like the Pomona Valley during the Civil Rights era bonded through common experiences and challenges. Families like the Johnsons, the Weavers, and the Branches on Avalon and the Halls and the Woodses on Belinda were each others' backup. Still, these homes were our pieces of the rock, and we valued them as such. Those of us who were the offspring of this settling by Depression-era parents may not have recognized it at the time, but we were inhabitants of a neighborhood in the midst of a demographic shift. It coalesced into a community that launched a generation of successful adults, who in turn have become parents and moved to other communities to raise their kids and grandkids. We were the beneficiaries of the surviving, striving, thriving ethos of our parents. To differing degrees, our parents scraped and scratched to have a nice house in a nice neighborhood near good schools. Sintown was that for us back in the day.

We lived in Sintown 'cause Daddy worked at the Hughes Aircraft Ground System campus in Fullerton. He had to drive the two-lane Brea Canyon Road between Pomona and Fullerton every day. This daily sojourn begs the question of why we didn't just move to an area in North Orange County, closer to his work. Daddy had done some house-hunting on his lunch hour, but couldn't even find a realtor who would work with him. They'd hear his precise, correct English on the phone and his exotic name, "Clovis Bordeaux," and know they had an excellent customer. Once they saw him, all of a sudden there weren't any houses to show and no prospects on the horizon. He never got any callbacks. The truth is, in '64 with Proposition 14 and the California Real Estate Association (CREA), North Orange County was not a very welcoming place for black folks, and Momma was just not up for the daily struggle of encountering and navigating prejudice and discrimination. She had faced down some seriously racist situations back home while growing up in the Ville, the segregated North End of St. Louis, Missouri. Momma always said that St. Louis was a small town that wanted to be a big city. She called her hometown "Up

South" because even though it was north of the Mason-Dixon Line, it had all the laws, mores, traditions, and customs of any southern city. The case that became the Supreme Court's Dred Scott Decision originated in St. Louis. Momma and her family had encountered racist store owners, bus drivers, and politicians—everyday rednecks in St. Louis—and she was not about to put her family through that ugliness here in California. She figured that the transition from Catholic school to public school for her three oldest boys would be hard enough without them being the "one and only" in their classes.

Momma and Daddy had a keen sense of the social changes that were occurring around them. They were acutely aware of the crushing segregation and racial discrimination they grew up with while hurrying to take advantage of the benefits of getting an education, working hard at your job, and utilizing the American system of home ownership. But none of their preparations in trying to shield their boys from the more virulent forms of a racist society worked completely. I had experiences from the time we landed in Sintown that showed me I was an "other." These experiences taught me that my friends and I were growing up in a different Pomona from the projected suburban image and, in a larger sense, a different America that had different rules and different expected outcomes for colored kids.

I am sure these experiences repeat themselves a lot across this country. Many Black Americans can recite the time they first encountered personal racism aimed specifically at them. I remember an episode with Ralph, my first friend in Pomona. He and his family lived down Avalon, on the other side of the street. We had met at the park, watching a little league game, and just started hangin' out. He lived with his mother, stepfather, and two younger sisters.

When Ralph and I heard that Lurch was gonna be at Unimart, we went nuts. We were huge fans of the "Addams Family" TV show, and Lurch was our favorite character. Morticia was a very close second in a horny, twelve-year-old-boy kinda way. Lurch had only one line in the entire show, "You rang?", but he said it every episode. We could get an autographed picture if we were one of the first twenty-five kids at the store at eleven o'clock on Saturday. I got up early to get my chores done so we could be at the front of the line., Ralph was waiting in his driveway when I came down Avalon. He glided into the street and fell in beside me as we rode along. When we got to the store, we saw some folding tables with big cutout pictures next to them. One was of the Addams family with Uncle Fester, Wednesday, Thing, and the rest. The other was of the Addams's spooky old mansion. There were two guys standing behind the table, and judging by his size, one of them was Lurch. Only a few other kids were waiting, so we were sure we were going to get an autographed picture.

We quickly locked up our bikes and got in line. The closer we got to Lurch, the less impressed we were. First off, the actor who played him, Ted Cassidy, was a tall dude, but we thought Lurch was a hulking giant! Second, it gets hot in Pomona, and this poor guy's make-up was starting to run. Finally, the "autographed picture" was one of a bazillion that was being handed out to anyone passing by. We took ours and ran into the store.

We headed straight for the toy section—the only reason to even have a store like this, in my opinion. We dove into the model cars and G.I. Joe's and the like. When I saw the "Man from U.N.C.L.E." display, I was on those toys instantly. They were based on the TV series spies, who had all these gadgets where one thing turned into another. I picked up a black plastic camera that, at the push of a couple of secret buttons, turned into a revolver! There were an attaché case and a gun holster that strapped under your armpit. I got Ralph's attention and play-shot him a couple of times. After a while, we picked up our autographed pictures and headed for the store exit.

Just as we got through the door, two big, beefy guys stepped in our way. They were wearing jeans and faded blue polo shirts with some kind of logo over the left breast. One of them had a walkie-talkie on his belt that kept belching incomprehensible dialog every twenty or thirty seconds. "Come with us," he said. Ralph looked at me; his eyes were calm. I think he thought this was an adventure. But I was scared to death, even though I knew I had to done nothing wrong. I was absolutely sure Daddy would kill me for being picked up in a store. Then Momma would dig me up and kill me again. The guys walked us through the store, taking us down a main aisle like they had apprehended a two-kid crime wave. One said something into the walkie-talkie and then said, "Over." People were looking at Ralph and me like we were on our way to getting whatever was coming to us. I heard a lady tell one of the guys to "show 'em who's boss."

We were taken to a small room in one of the store's back corners. There were two raggety folding chairs and a beat up institutional table. We were told to sit down. Then they left and closed the door. Every awful interrogation movie I had ever seen started running through my mind. Ralph just sat there, looking at his tennis shoes. He did not seem at all agitated. I wondered if maybe it was not the first time this had happened to him. Finally, he said, "Don't worry. They're just trying to scare you."

"What did we do? I didn't do anything!" I protested.

"Doesn't matter. If they want you to get in trouble, you're gonna get in trouble."

I fell silent until the men came back. The one with the Walkie-talkie stood opposite me and leaned against the wall like he had been given the assignment to hold it up. He just looked at me silently for three or four minutes while that dang walkie-talkie squawked. In a matter-of-fact voice, he asked me what I had done with the camera. For a split second, I didn't understand the question., He saw the confusion on my face and repeated the question. "What did you do with the camera? We saw you playing with it."

"If you saw us playing with it, then you saw us put it down." blurted Ralph.

"I'm not talking to you, boy."

"I don't have any camera. I put it down." I said with as much bravado as I could muster.

They left again, as suddenly as they had come. After about five minutes, the one without the Walkie-talkie returned and said we could go. He gave us a perfunctory speech about how the security team had its eye on us and this, that, and the other. He escorted us out of the store, making a show of catching a couple of juvenile delinquents, even if we hadn't actually done anything. We unlocked our bikes and left the autographed pictures on the ground near the bike rack. We rode home in silence. Ralph peeled off when we got to his driveway. I went home and had some grapes and watched the Wide World of Sports. The Globetrotters were going to be on later. I never told Momma and Daddy about Lurch or the camera, and Ralph and I never talked about it either.

This kind of treatment did not stop with harassing two little kids. Sometimes it was a family affair. Momma liked shopping at Unimart, a membership store for government employees. It had a grocery store with lower prices than both Alpha Beta and Safeway, and the meat and produce seemed to be of better quality. She involved all four of us. She would divide her list in two and give half of it to my brothers, who would take a cart and ramble down the aisles, arguing over who got to push it. I stayed with Momma, grabbing items at her instructions. The truth is, nobody needed a list 'cause we got the same things every week. Momma liked brand names for some things, but she would go store brands in a minute if it looked like a good buy. As junior shoppers, we knew what we could put in the cart and what would get a dismissive look and a stern, "Put that back."

Cereal was a weekly skirmish. We wanted the sweetest, crunchiest cereal you could get—Fruit Loops or Frosted Flakes. Momma would have none of this. She had four big mouths to feed, and her solution was a Super-Duper, Extra Large bag of Puffed Rice. The bag it came in was taller than me. Puffed Rice was a slightly sweet, cardboard-textured cereal that barely met that low bar of being called cereal. It was supposed to be air-puffed kernels of rice, but these things had mutated. You could not sink the kernels; they just sat on top of the milk.

Momma liked to pick out the meat and produce, which taught me a couple of things, cooking-wise. Momma always had to buy cuts of meat for six, so she would concoct recipes that could survive three or four rounds of leftovers. One roast would supply two dinners, a round of sandwiches and finally a batch of hash with onions, potatoes, and gravy. Choosing good fruits and vegetables was crucially important in our house. We enjoyed our plums and peaches and melons and apples. The person who picked out lousy fruit for our family would be talked about all day long. I felt pretty good, cause I learned to pick perfect produce. Jude, Sammy, and Visey ran around the store getting canned goods, bread, frozen foods and the like.

On one of these shopping trips, Jude was pushing the other cart when we met at the checkout stand. The Bordeaux boys had a special way of transferring the food and groceries from cart to conveyor belt. Jude would grab stuff from the basket and toss it to Visey to place on the belt. Sammy's OCD kicked in, and he arranged all the cans by size and type. Bread, eggs, and chips were always last.

Momma had trained us all well, so she had proceeded to write her check and get out her driver's licenses and State Employee card. She was tired and, although we were helpful, we were a handful. She just wanted to get these groceries home and put away so she could sit down. As all the groceries were being checked through, Momma noticed that the items were being pushed down the checkout counter a little too forcefully. She asked the clerk to stop throwing her groceries. The woman stared at my mother with a bored and uninterested look. Nothing irked my mother more than not being taken seriously. She quickly completed and signed her check and handed the check and ID's over; the clerk looked over the check and, without looking up, asked my mother to pronounce her name. This inquiry annoyed Momma because she had been shopping here for over a year and no one had ever asked her to say her name. She wearily said, "Bordeaux. Bernice Bordeaux."

The clerk then said, "That's fancy. What kind of name is that for a Negro?"

Momma was stunned. We all noticed a tensing of her body as she leaned into the clerk. We feared the worst. Momma's breathing was quickening, and an asthma attack was right around the corner. We were scared she was about to get sick AND go off on this woman. Instead, she calmly told the clerk that it was her name and she was going to take her name and her check and leave this store, which she did. "No one has ever asked me to explain my name!" She gathered the four of us and made a bee-line for the nearest exit. We had no idea what had just happened. We were walking out of the store, and our groceries were still on the checkout stand. Momma was striding toward our black Ford station wagon in no mood to answer our silly questions. Instead, once we were all in the car, she turned to us in the back seat and said, "I can't explain all the reasons I left that store. But I can tell you that I will never let an uneducated grocery checker question who or what I am. You'll understand one day."

When we got home, Daddy asked where the groceries were. All four of us simultaneously tried to tell the story, complete with action and sound effects. Momma quickly quieted the peanut gallery and calmly recounted what had happened at Unimart. Daddy's expression did not change. Instead, he just pulled Momma close and hugged her. "You did the right thing," he said quietly. "We won't be shopping at Unimart anymore."

Catholic School

WHEN I WAS in the third grade, I once saw Daddy writing a check. I asked what he was doing, and he said he was paying tuition with this check and that it was just like money. Momma and Daddy believed in the miracle of compound interest and had always taught us to save our money. Each of us had passbooks at the local bank. They had explained the difference between and savings and checking accounts to Sammy, Jude, and Visey. All I knew was that they were different.

He went on to tell me what tuition was and why he was paying it. At that time, all four of us were enrolled at St. Joachim Catholic School on the South Side in Chicago. I think they paid full pop for Sammy and Jude and got a percentage break on Visey and me. Whatever the case, they were paying a significant nut every month to educate us because Momma and Daddy believed in the quality of Catholic school education. In their eyes, almost any Catholic school was going to deliver a better basic educational foundation than any public school. Momma especially felt this way because she taught in both public and private settings and knew their strengths and weaknesses. This dedication to Catholic education continued when we came to California. Visey and I attended one Catholic school and then another while we lived in Compton. Sammy and Jude were put in the first classes of the newly opened Catholic boy's high school.

In Pomona, I attended the sixth and seventh grades at St. Joseph's on Holt Avenue. I know it was a gorgeous campus with a mission-style church and school buildings; a convent and rectory; a swimming pool and athletic fields. But I remember little else—only certain vignettes about the school and the people. I do recollect that I was the "one and only."

Well, St. Joseph was on the main drag in the middle of town. 1964 was before carpools and "helicopter parents" constantly hovering over their kids. Momma and Daddy had Sammy and Jude at Ganesha High, Visey was at Marshall Junior High, and I was at St. Joseph. They were both working—Momma teaching 3rd Grade in the West Covina School District and Daddy in the Ground Systems Section at Hughes Aircraft in Fullerton. The thought of driving me to school never crossed their minds. That's why God made bicycles.

To this time, I had attended four Catholic schools in three cities in two states, so I consistently received excellent elementary instruction. The downside was the isolation of always being the new kid (which continued even when I finally went to public school in the eighth grade), and a growing distance between my brothers and myself. Sammy and Jude were about to begin their post-high school lives, with Sammy moving into an apartment when he went to Mt. SAC Community College, and Jude went to Daddy's alma mater, Lincoln University in Jefferson City, Missouri. Visey would soon go to live with Aunt Juanita and Uncle Ivan in St. Louis because he and Momma were not getting along. By the time I was in eighth grade at Marshall Junior High, I was a de facto only child. And I was in public school only because of what happened toward the end of my seventh-grade year.

As I said, I had been the "one and only" at St. Joseph. For the uninitiated, this refers to being the one and only Negro child in any given group or organization. I had never had that particular experience before and, at first, I wasn't even aware of it. With a few exceptions, I didn't have any friends, and I wasn't chosen to play in any of the games on the yard at recess. I was the new kid, and nobody ever picks the new kid. Class work was not an issue for me because Momma was a teacher and Daddy accepted no excuses when it came to grades. I thought I was just another uniform in just another class. It didn't dawn on me that I was different from other kids because, to me, we all looked the same: charcoal grey pants, white shirts, and blue sweaters.

Toward the end of my seventh-grade year, I was ready for summer vacation. I didn't really like St. Joseph. I had endured two years of kids not wanting to sit by me in class or in the cafeteria. I seldom was called on, although when I was, my answers were right. I was on the swimming team, but I couldn't crack the small groups of kids who had been in school together since first grade.

Maybe it says something that I only remember one or two kids from that time. One kid, in particular, made sure I remembered him—a classmate whose father was an actor on a popular TV show. Dad was a quasi-celebrity so, ergo, the son was a quasi-celebrity. But he was a punk. And he was a bully. And I was one of his favorite targets.

I didn't play much basketball, even though I had some skills I learned playing with my brothers. I didn't understand soccer (still don't) and I couldn't hit a baseball if it were sitting on a tee. That left football. Now when I was younger, I was a big kid. I did all my growing early. I was bigger than most of the kids in my class, so I could block and stuff like that. But blockers don't get to touch the football, and that's half the fun. Of course, celebrity-boy always had to be the quarterback. When I suggested that, perhaps, I could also throw a pass, he got indignant. He argued that I was too slow. He had a point: I was slow. But it was the principle of the thing.

During one of the few basketball games I played in, that same kid fouled me hard enough to knock me down. I invoked the rules I played under on our court at home and called a foul. He went off. First, he swore he didn't touch me and accused me of not knowing how to play. He claimed he was going for the ball and barely touched me. Then he called me a sissy. That got the other kids on the court revved up. Then he called me a nigger.

It was so unexpected that I almost didn't react. Although I had heard the word before, it was the first time it had been directed at me. I wasn't even sure I knew what it meant. I did know that it was bad. I put my head down and rushed him so hard we both tumbled to the ground. Before I knew it, I was head-locking and holding him so he couldn't get a good swing at me. I remember thinking all those tag-team wrestling matches my brothers and I used to have were paying off. I had the upper hand, but somehow I knew I was about to be in big trouble.

Sure enough, a huge hand grabbed me by my shirt collar and lifted me off the kid like one of those crane machines. I knew something was up when I was the only one taken to the principal's office. The principal didn't know what to do. She gave me a stern talking-to, but I didn't know why. When she asked me to explain myself, I laid the story out and waited for justice to be done. Justice turned out to be a one-day "cooling-off" period. I would be allowed to come to school on Monday, but I would have to sit next to Sister Mary Gregory all day, even during recess and lunch. Worse yet, my reputation as a troublemaker was set.

Momma didn't hide her fury over this; that meek little me had been in a fight disappointed and angered her. Since this incident happened on a Friday, I got an entire Saturday of being called a "thug," "hoodlum" and "heathen." She was mortified that the one black child in the whole damn school, her son, got in a fight. She made it clear that I had let the family down. I complained that celebrity-boy had started the fight when he shoved me and started calling me names. Momma turned to me on a dime and said in an almost pleading voice, "You think you're the first colored boy to be called a nigger? You can't go around fighting everybody who hates you." I knew fighting was bad, but I could tell that this was bigger than just a fight. I went to bed on Saturday completely confused.

A funny thing happened on Sunday morning. We got up like we always did and went to eight o'clock mass. Usually, there was a hum to the house, a vibe that had Sammy and Jude bickering and Visey noodling on the piano as he always did. Momma would be heard singing, "He's got the whole world in his hands." But not this Sunday. The quiet was more than everybody trying to stay out of the line of fire. There was a seriousness that I couldn't really understand.

I soon witnessed something I have never forgotten. No one said a word on the drive to mass. Imagine Momma, Daddy, and four normally rambunctious boys in a '62 Rambler Ambassador riding in absolute silence. Daddy found a parking space, and we piled out. He made sure we all had our missals and locked the car. He then grasped Momma's hand and led us into the church. We all dipped our fingers in holy water and made the sign of the cross. We started walking down the center aisle; this was unusual because Daddy normally led us down the right side aisle.

As we walked, Sammy, Jude, Visey, and I could see people pointing at us and murmuring. Momma and Daddy stared straight ahead. The four of us were ready to stop at our regular middle pew, but Momma and Daddy kept walking. Her grip on his hand was firm and resolute. The pointing and whispering subsided. Daddy walked us to the front of the church, as close to the altar as we could get. As we genuflected, a couple had to move down so the six of us could sit. They moved to the other end of the pew. I was glad when mass started because it felt like the attention would finally be off us, me.

Momma had me sitting right next to her. As the mass moved along through all the standing, kneeling, and sitting, I noticed that Daddy and Momma stood taller and spoke more clearly during prayers and sang the hymns with more emotion than normal. I, in turn, stood up straighter, and prayed and sang louder. When communion time came, the six of us walked up as a single unit, a family. When we got back to the pew, Momma reached over and squeezed my hand. After mass, we walked straight to the car. Nobody said much, even when we stopped at the little German pastry shop at Five Points. This shop had the best strudel and stopping to get a coffee cake for breakfast after Mass was a regular thing.

We went home and had a "Big Breakfast." I don't mean to say we had a big breakfast, although we certainly did. I mean we had a "BIG Breakfast." In the Bordeaux house, that meant bacon, biscuits, fried apples, eggs, juice, coffee, strawberries, cantaloupe, and coffee cake. Usually, this was a rowdy affair with everybody pitching in to set the table, slice the apples, make the biscuits, etc. After we got out of our church clothes, we started to get everything ready. All preparation activity was timed around Daddy cooking the perfect griddle of bacon and eggs, sunny-side up for everyone. We had to have the table set and be ready to say the blessing when he delivered the first round of eggs. He might have broken a few yolks in his time, but I never saw them. And even though we still ate good, this Sunday was different. The normal bickering and chatter were absent.

The whole day went like this. There was a calm not normally present in our house. Momma and Daddy kinda' left us to our own devices. Sammy, Jude, and Visey went to play basketball. I was thinking about Monday and sitting by Sister Mary Gregory and not looking forward to it. I was mad; I was the only one to be punished. It occurred to me that celebrity-boy would be sitting in his normal seat and I'd have to sit there and look at him all day. After Ed Sullivan and Bonanza, I went to bed.

In a house with four boys going to three schools, Monday mornings can be a riot. Daddy was always out of the house by 6:30 to make his way through Brea Canyon to Hughes Aircraft in Fullerton. But, this Monday was different. He was still home, and we acted accordingly; we toned down the arguments and conflicts. If anything, we tried to stay out of Daddy's way, because if he was still home when he should have been at work, he was not going to be in the mood for any foolishness. I was about to get on my bike and pedal to school, but he told me to go wait in the car. Sammy and Jude tumbled out of the house, followed by Visey, all on their way to school as usual.

After a few minutes, Daddy came out, started the car and pulled off down the street. At first, I thought I had been pardoned, and he was taking me to work with him. Instead, he got into the left turn lane at Five Points and headed east down Holt toward St. Joseph. Daddy had never taken me to school. This was uncharted territory. I had no idea what to expect, but I could not imagine that it would be good for me.

Once Daddy parked the car, he sat silent for a moment. He looked straight ahead and took a deep breath. Then he got out of the car and walked me toward the school office. When we entered, he told me to sit down and announced himself to the secretary as if he was expected. He sat down next to me in the only other chair, and we waited in silence. In just a few minutes, we went into the principal's office. The principal said good morning and adjusted her nun's habit as she sat. She opened the conversation by saying how sorry she was for this whole incident. Daddy held up his right hand with his palm toward the principal, gently interrupting her. My eyes locked onto that hand.

When he spoke, his voice was clear. Daddy was an engineer and a physicist. He thought and spoke in very precise terms. "You think this started when Jacques hit the other kid. That's why you only brought him into your office. The other boy called my son a nigger. He says he tried to tell you that but was embarrassed to say the word. He also said you wouldn't listen to him."

SINTOWN SAINTS

The principal sat stoically, but I saw her flinch when Daddy said the word. From my seat, I could see his eyes, and as he spoke, they narrowed. "We pay tuition here because we value the education your school promotes. Our kids have always attended Catholic schools. But I do not like what you taught Jacques with this 'incident.' So we're going to stop paying tuition here. Friday will be Jacques' last day at St. Joseph. Please prorate the tuition and issue a refund. And...he will not be returning for next year." The principal tried to speak, but Daddy had said what he came to say. He and Momma had talked about this between the two of them and decided that I was not coming back to St. Joseph's. I guess that explains all the quiet at home.

Daddy rose to his feet and thanked the principal for her time. He turned to me like an usher and said, "Let's go." We walked out of the office and did not look back. I tried to mimic every move Daddy made. He unlocked the car and told me to get in. It had gotten warm and stuffy inside the car. As soon as the door closed, he spoke. "You'll go to Marshall next year. Then all four of you will be in public school." There was a sadness in his voice because he felt the education was better in a Catholic school, and now he was walking away from it. "How long do you have before summer vacation?" "'Bout a week and a half," I answered.

"I want you to finish a big chore a day until vacation. Start with cleaning the garage today; scrub both of the showers tomorrow; cut the grass; stay busy. Pick a book and finish it by that time, too."

He went quiet. When he turned to me again, he had a dull look in his eyes. "You can't fight every ignorant clown who calls you a name. That boy was showing his ignorance, and you got punished for it. There are some fights you just are not going to win." I looked at him and nodded my understanding although I knew I only got a part of what he was saying. We were quiet as he drove me home.

Connections

NINTH GRADE WAS the pinnacle year of my athletic career. I was on the Track & Field team at Marshall Junior High. I competed in the long jump and 660, which was basically a lap and a half—too long to be a sprint and certainly not cross- country. Perfect for a plodder like me. I felt pretty good as I joined my partners after the track meet. We had just beaten Palomares Junior High, and Reggie had run a strong 100. Keith and Ronald had dominated the long jump. I had run my best time in the 660, so I got a ribbon. I came out of the locker room and caught up with the fellas going south on Ganesha toward Five-Points. We visited the Alpha Beta Supermarket after most meets for snacks and sodas. That's a polite way of saying we grabbed cold cuts and cheese, potato chips, Fritos, cookies, juice, and sodas. We even paid for some of it.

We were headed back down the street, toward Sintown. Ronald and Reggie were wolfin' on one another; trading verbal jabs and playing the dozens. Meanwhile, Keith, all elbows and knees, was selling tickets and goading them on as he laughed non-stop. "You gonna let him say that?!" "Daaaaang!" Keith was a walking perpetual-motion machine. He was tall, with arms so long, we swore he could scratch his knees without bending down. He had this *basso profundo* voice that boomed even when he whispered. When we got to Arroyo, we crossed Ganesha and finished our grub. We were busting up at almost everything that was said. One of the fellas was describing a particularly fervent slow-jam grind at a recent garage party. All of us knew who he was talking about 'cause we had all been ground into submission by this sister — a life-changing experience for a ninth grader. We crossed over the wash and hit Avalon. Those of us going into Sintown made the turn. Ronald continued across the street toward Ganesha Hills. He had a pretty good hike ahead of him.

My house was the fifth one from the corner on the left, so I peeled off first. I was preoccupied with having gotten a ribbon and the jokes and woof-tickets Keith had been dishin' out. At that moment, I figured life didn't get any better. As I neared the house, I saw both cars in the driveway. Daddy usually put his car in the garage, so he must've been in a hurry to get in the house. I put my key in the front door and opened it. The only sound I heard was a somber narrator on the TV. As I walked down the short entryway, I saw Daddy first. He was still wearing his work clothes: slacks, short-sleeved white shirt, tie. Momma was sitting on the couch, motionless. They were staring at CBS News in some kind of shock. I saw tears on their faces. I was confused as to what was going on, but when I finally focused on the reporter I heard the words, "Dr. Martin Luther King Junior has been killed." The screen showed a hotel balcony with some people standing there pointing across a field at a tenement.

I stood there frozen. I had seen Momma and Daddy in this state after President Kennedy. After Medgar Evers. After Malcolm X. After Bobby Kennedy. After Emmitt Till. After four little girls. After Bloody Sunday. At that moment, in my mind, I began to put together the non-randomness of these events. All of a sudden, I felt very tired with the weight of the events unfolding in front of us.

It would be more than an understatement to say simply that Martin Luther King was a great man. But at that time, I didn't know much more than that he was revered by my parents and most of the adults in my world. And I knew the Civil Rights movement was serious business because we had heard regular reports of demonstrations, lynchings, bombings, and murders. This murder, however, was the first time I felt like it was a man I knew something about. In the following days, I watched as a vibrant and growing freedom movement and the Poor People's Campaign stumbled and became unsure of their footing. Dr. King had been an authentic hero and statesman in Daddy's eyes. Momma had always feared for him and believed in the inevitability of his death. She thought if the Klan would kill little girls, Dr. King and the people around him might as well have had targets on their chests. Now he was gone. Black communities all over the country were seething and ready to explode. Civil disturbances and riots would flare up as anger and anguish prevailed and was invariably met with para-military force.

What I saw of America in the days after Dr. King's murder changed me. I heard my people referred to as everything but Americans. Anything that passed as commentary reflected an acute ignorance of huge portions of the American population. Newspapers and television outlets were scrambling to find ways of explaining the confusion and chaos, but what was shown instead was their myopia born of years of dismissing and overlooking these communities. In L.A, you could've counted on one hand the number of in-depth stories about the city south of the Santa Monica Freeway before the assassination. There were no reporters who knew these parts of the city and there were certainly no editors between the two major dailies, the Times, and the Herald-Examiner. Political and economic power resided in other parts of Southern California, not in South Central.

I mark my understanding of all of the debates that fueled the social upheaval around me from Dr. King's assassination. Prior to that, I had heard the discussions among our elders about the different factions, strategies, personalities and events of the Civil Rights movement. What I did not have was a context for all of the turmoil I saw. I was in suburban California, not Selma. I did not make the connection between the struggle in Mississippi and my life in Pomona. All of a sudden, with the assassination of this warrior, and my parent's reaction to it, I saw the connections.

I realized that our family had somehow beaten the odds. I had always been aware of the material differences between us and some of those around us. These differences existed within our family also. But now I could see the inescapable connection between me and every other Negro in America: we were all at risk, regardless of where we lived or what we did. I had never considered myself special in any way when I was a kid. I spent much of my time trying not to be noticed. Suddenly, I began to think about some new, broader issues and talk about them with Jay and Ronald and some of the other Fellas. I picked up some books on our people's history and literature, and conversations with Momma and Daddy took on a more social, political tone. Being introduced to these topics amidst the tumult of 1968 heightened my sense of connection to the men and women of my extended family and the elders in my friend's families. I began to see my uncles and aunts as "soldiers" among the thousands of Black people who had been enlisted in the frontlines of the fight for equality through the NAACP (National Association for the Advancement of Colored People), SCLC (Southern Christian Leadership Conference), CORE (Congress of Racial Equality) or SNCC (Student Non-Violent Coordinating Committee.) And it finally came to me that I really couldn't opt out of this fight. So many before me had paid so much as to make any unwillingness to join the battle for inclusion close to betrayal. My connection to them was their legacy and my birthright.

THE CAMPAIGN

IN THE FALL of 1968, I was in my third year of public school after seven years of private, Catholic education. I was a square peg in a round hole. I had buck teeth, big ears, and wore glasses. I was in the Audio-Visual class in junior high school. I wasn't an athlete, although I gave it my best shot. The problem was that I had no talent. My jump shot was neither. I couldn't dance—not like the kids I saw at Sock-Hops

Jacques as sophomore class president, Ganesha High School, 1968.

at Marshall. I didn't really know anybody because, although I had lived in Sintown for two years, I had only ridden past Marshall on the way to St. Joseph's. When I came to Marshall, I was promptly enrolled in advanced, gifted classes. This was great, but it removed me even further from a comfortable social circle. However, this is where I first met James, Ronald, Debra, Richard, Malcolm and a few others who I hold close to this day. But after all was said and done, I was a geeky nerd.

When I answered the door one Saturday afternoon in the fall of '68, I was aware of national political events like the Civil Rights Movement, the Viet Nam War, and Johnson and Nixon. But I didn't know anything about the local school board election coming up. It was James at the door asking me if I wanted to help him throw flyers for his dad. Now, I kinda knew James, but just barely. We had some classes together and maybe played some basketball, but we weren't yet on a first-name basis or anything. Further, I didn't know his dad and didn't know what "throwing flyers" meant. Even so, I called out to Momma and Daddy in the kitchen, "I'm going out, I'll be back in a little while."

When we got out in the driveway, James jumped into the back of a flatbed truck stacked with hundreds of folded pamphlets endorsing Dr. James Bell for a

seat on the school board. There were pictures of Dr. Bell with his trademark muttonchops sideburns, and short natural, and the word "VOTE" in big, bold letters. Another guy in the truck named Johnny told me that throwing flyers meant driving slowly up and down every street in west, south, and north Pomona pitching pamphlets into every yard until they were all gone. Each of them had to be rolled and rubber-banded, so we were pretty busy in the bed of that truck.

Dr. James Bell, circa 1972

At first, we worked silently, but soon we were singing along with the R & B coming out of the truck radio. James and I started comparing groups and singers that we liked, with him doing little snippet imitations of Eddie Kendricks or Sly Stone. We soon discovered we were both Catholic school survivors, him from Norfolk, Virginia and me from all over. I had three older brothers; he had one older and one baby sister. His mother was a nurse and mine was a teacher. His Pops was an administrator at Cal Poly. Mine was an engineer at Hughes Aircraft. We talked about teachers we liked and those we disliked at school and embarrassingly compared notes on the girls we thought were fine. Johnny was a student at Mt. Sac who said Dr. Bell was helping him transfer to Cal Poly. He endorsed some of our musical favorites but was too busy plotting which route to take with the driver to pay serious attention to our adolescent chatter.

We had started our trek through Pomona by driving through Sintown. We went down Avalon and made the curve onto Cromwell and then left onto Canterbury. We continued, zig-zagging our way down Carlton, Belinda, Concord, Academy, and Farrington. We threw a flyer into each yard and barked at whoever we saw to "VOTE BELL FOR SCHOOL BOARD!" Most everyone was good-natured about it and at least looked at the flyer. There were some looks of recognition for Johnny and James or the guy driving the truck.

When we finished with Sintown, we headed to the Islands in north Pomona. This was the first time I saw the other Black neighborhoods, and they were almost identical in the small tract houses in neighborhoods set close to a high school. The Islands were adjacent to Pomona High School, just as Sintown wrapped around Ganesha. Periodically, we would pull up to a barbershop, beauty parlor, or corner store and James would jump out of the truck and run into the store with a handful of pamphlets. He would come running out empty handed. As we drove through, throwing pamphlets and calling out to people to vote, I heard the word "precinct" and recognized it from my parents' conversations about Chicago politics. It was repeated when we drove down to the Flats and the Village in south Pomona. We covered these precincts in the same systematic way we worked Sintown and the Islands.

We finished tossing the flyers in the Village just as the sun was setting. I realized I had walked out of the house in just my t-shirt, and it was starting to get cold. Johnny and the driver decided it was time to call it a day. We headed to an office on Garey, just north of Holt near my doctor's office. When the truck was parked, James and I jumped down and went into the office. The space inside was sparsely furnished with desks and file cabinets. Boxes and more pamphlets seemed to be everywhere. James went over to a big guy in the middle of a group and said a few words. I noticed that Dr. Plummer, our family doctor, was in the group. Matter of fact, everyone in that group seemed to be of a professional type; lots of ties and long-sleeve white shirts. In a minute, the man came over to me and introduced himself as James Bell, Sr. I shook his hand and said "Hi." He thanked me for all my hard work but I just kinda grinned. He told me to help myself to some pizza.

After a while, I noticed it was dark outside and I realized Momma was going to kill me because I had been gone all afternoon without even a phone call. I asked James if he could help me get a ride home. He told me his father was going to be leaving in a minute and he would drop me off. In short order, we were cruising down the street in Dr. Bell's "houseboat" station wagon. We rode through Pomona without saying much. I thanked Dr. Bell for the ride, and he chuckled in a way I would hear a million times over the years and said, "No, thank YOU!"

James could have knocked on a lot of fellas' doors, but he picked mine, and to this day, I don't know why. I do know that I learned so much about so many different things that I mark much of my understanding of the world from that day. I learned that if you want someone's vote, you have to ask for it; work for it. I learned how the neighborhoods in even small-town Pomona had been carved up through redlining and not-so-subtle manipulations by bankers and realtors so that there were very specific parts of the city where we could live. I learned that Dr. Bell was trying to become the first Black member of the school board. I learned that even though we canvassed three different parts of the city, there were homeowners and hard-working people in each precinct who just wanted the best for their kids. I learned that there were a lot of Black families in Pomona that had moved out to the suburbs for jobs and cheap housing just like my parents. I even learned about some of the issues in the election. Of course, the greatest learning that day was the way a deep friendship that persists to this day was formed while throwing those flyers.

Now, more than fifty years later, I call James my best friend on the planet after my wife. We took a teenage road trip adventure together, camping in Yosemite and discovering San Francisco and the surrounding Bay Area with serious music and conversations about our places in the world. He always knew he was going to become a lawyer and had been pointing in that direction throughout high school and college. I had not yet developed any coherent plan about my future, but Jay would later attend the University of San Francisco School of

Law and make The City his home. He was in my wedding, and he helped me bury my father. I have officiated both of his parent's memorial services. We have lived vicariously through each other's successes and disappointments. More importantly, we share so much history and humor, sense of social justice and the skeptical optimism of black men in America who believe, as a nation, we can and should do better.

I love me some Jay Bell. He is my definition of a friend.

BEETLES

CARS WEREN'T A huge part of my growing up, but when I woke up and connected wheels to mobility and teenage freedom, it was all over. I had my permit within two days of my 15-and-a-half "birthday" in June. Daddy had been letting me drive short distances and tutoring me on the finer points, and my sophomore class schedule included Driver's Ed.

Daddy's '65 Bug. I learned to drive a stick in this car.

I had always paid attention to how Daddy operated our beige '65 Volkswagen differently than the Pontiac Tempest station wagon. The Tempest had an automatic transmission, but the VW had a "stick," a manual transmission. I watched the drivers in my family manage the gas, the brakes, the rear views and the blinkers in our automatic. But the VW Bug, for such a simple little car, had all that AND a clutch and stick. I have always thought a stick engaged the driver more in the driving process. Done correctly, driving a stick, working the clutch, on top of the regular driving chores, just made me feel more like a driver.

The VW was a massive cultural phenomenon at the time. Bugs were everywhere. Disney made movies about the car. Print ads and commercials for it were simple and clever. The car's utilitarian ugliness was its greatest asset. It could be anything to anybody. Everything about the car was Spartan and to my eyes—ugly. The fenders, bumpers, and most everything else was interchangeable. It had a four-stroke engine that whined when you drove in first gear and sipped gas. It was small and it got you from point A to point B. If you expand the idea of a Volkswagen to include all of its models like squarebacks, busses, Karmann Ghias, dune buggies, and the Thing; Volkswagens were simply all over the place.

But what made the Bug was its adaptability. James had traded in his gas-guzzling '65 Mustang for a powder-blue '69 Bug, which he immediately outfitted with headers, big rear tires, and bigger fiberglass fenders. Sweet and stylish Valerie had a brown-mustard colored Karmann Ghia that fit her to a tee. Freddie's blue bug somehow just looked faster 'cause of the way he drove. Ralph had his "painted" with a blue and gold velvet-like coating that caused the Fellas to name his car the Fuzz-Bug. After he neglected it and wouldn't pay the ducats to have his car "shampooed," the car got filthy, and the name morphed into the Fungus-Bug.

Daddy had traded in his red '62 Rambler Ambassador and bought the used '65 VW to get him back and forth from Pomona to Hughes Aircraft in Fullerton. Before the 57 Freeway was built, he was driving Brea Canyon Road between Five Points and Imperial Highway and needed a smaller, more economical car. He fell in love with that car. So much so that when Sammy needed a car, Daddy bought him a '69 VW. And when Visey called from St. Louis and said he needed a car he could transport his music equipment in, Daddy bought him a used VW hatchback. He completely bought into the humble "Beetle" or "Bug" version of the Volkswagen. Hook, line, and sinker.

Anyway, I took the preparation for getting my driver's license seriously. In those days, Mr. Trevino taught Driver's Ed. In addition to rules of the road, we were taught the inner workings of a car so we could tell the difference between a lug nut and a spark plug. We watched safe-driving films like "Blood on the Blacktop" that were meant to scare us into being good drivers. Instead, the corniness and awful film-making just increased our impatience. I, for one, couldn't wait to get behind the wheel.

Once we were finished with the classroom instruction, we went out on the road. I spent a couple of Fall Saturdays tooling around Pomona in a Student Driver car with an assistant football coach and two other students I didn't know. On one particular Saturday, I sat in the back seat, listening and watching as each of them forgot to put on their blinker or check their rearview mirrors. I swore I would remember these details when my turn came.

When we pulled into the parking lot at the 7-Eleven on Dudley, I climbed out of the back seat and took my place behind the wheel. I reached between my legs and adjusted the seat to my liking. I checked and adjusted my rear views. I looked at the coach, and he looked back at me. By the time he finally spoke, the discomfort from the two others trainees staring at the back of my head had me discombobulated. Coach asked me if I had forgotten anything. I raced through the sequence I had watched Momma, Daddy, Sammy, and Jude execute a million times before starting a car. I came up with the answer right after he said, "seat belt."

When Coach told me to pull out, I guided the car onto the street toward Orange Grove. We stayed in a residential neighborhood, and after a series of lefts and rights, lane changes, and four-way stops, Coach pointed back toward the school. He gave us some perfunctory comments about paying attention and staying focused. He finished his monologue just as we pulled up in front of the school. We said our goodbyes and I was on my way.

Daddy was in the driveway at 2124 when I walked up, and the VW was open on all fronts. He was cleaning out all of the stuff he had accumulated through the week. Now, for Daddy, "stuff" amounted to a bulletin from church and his bowling bag. He spent a lot of time in that car, and it just wasn't going to get junky.

He started closing lids, hoods, and doors and tossed me the keys. "We have some errands to run." I got in and ran through the sequence. Daddy's Bug was my car of choice in our family. Clo took pride in his car having the original equipment and being clean. This was a stick, and I was sure I could do this. I wasn't quite there on the clutch-gas-shift cha-cha, but I was trying not to grind any gears. Daddy was not watching me; he was staring straight ahead. I pulled out of the driveway and headed toward Ganesha. Daddy silently pointed right toward Five Points.

I thought we were heading over to Unimart; instead, he told me to turn east at Holt. East? I only knew left-right. I played it off like I had a clue and, on a hunch, prepared to turn left. When we got to the intersection, there was traffic at each of the streets, so we had to sit for a minute. Daddy asked me to predict the next green light. I had no idea what he was talking about. He said, "You have to know when it's your turn. And, when you're driving a car, you have to know where you are and where you're going."

I began watching the different lanes take their turns and was ready when our turn came. Daddy had fallen silent again. There was no radio. The VW only had an AM radio, and on Saturdays, there was nothing on that band Daddy wanted to hear. The only sounds between us were the whirr-and-shift of the four-stroke engine. Clo dug that sound. I thought it sounded like a pocketful of loose change. He had me pull into the Shell gas station on Holt. I parked next to the gas pump and sat there waiting for the pump jockey to come out. I couldn't wait to say, "fill 'er up." That's when Daddy said, looking straight ahead, "You take care of it."

He reached into the glove compartment and popped the little hatch covering the gas cap. Although I had pumped gas before, I had never purchased gas. I suddenly noticed the price: 29 cents a gallon. I had seen the young guys working at the station and mimicked what they had done. I checked the tires and scraped the squeegee across the windshield. The pump jockey servicing the next car over checked the oil, so I ran around to the back of the VW and found the dipstick. Of course, this was Clo's car. Tires, oil, windshield. Check, check, and check.

When the pump clicked off, I tried to get to a round number and got to exactly $2.25. Daddy made no motion toward his wallet. I soon got the hint: go pay the man. I should've seen this coming. Daddy was telling me to get used to paying for using his car. I had long heard Daddy and Momma rail against Jude, Sammy, and Visey about leaving one of their cars dirty or without any gas. Then and there I swore I was never going to be that kind of driver.

We continued down Holt. At every light and stop sign, I was aware that Clo was monitoring my driving and my shifting. Although he never looked at me, I knew he saw it all. How close was I to the car in front of me? How was my speed? Were my hands in the right positions? How was my cha-cha? I was a nervous wreck. When we got to Garey Avenue, Daddy pointed left and told me to go to Dr. Plummer's office. I kinda knew where the office was, even if I didn't know the address. At that time, Dr. Plummer was the only black physician in Pomona, and he was our family doctor. I had been to his office a ton because Momma made regular visits to manage her asthma. And I had just been in to get my football physical.

When I pulled in and parked, Clo gave me an envelope and told me to drop it through the mail slot. It had no street address, just "Dr. and Mrs. Plummer." I thought about what could have been in that envelope. It looked more like a letter than a bill. But then I wasn't paying a whole lot of bills at that time, so how would I know. Momma and Daddy knew the Plummers socially and attended some of the same Black civic events. Maybe the envelope had something to do with that. We left the Doctor's office and headed up Garey. Daddy told me to get in the left lane. As I was completing that maneuver, he blandly said, "I want you to get on the freeway. You're a pretty good driver. You can do it." He still hadn't looked at me.

I had never driven on a freeway. I wasn't sure this was the day I wanted to start. As we crossed Orange Grove, I stopped thinking of all the ways I could bail and started scoping out the oncoming traffic situation. I was going to have to make a left across traffic to get on the freeway. Up ahead, I could see just a couple of cars coming our way. I hit my blinker and moved to the far left lane. I waited for the two cars to pass and made my turn. I was on the transition road/freeway entrance, getting ready to shift into 3rd when this yellow Camaro comes barreling onto the freeway from McKinley and blasts past me without a second thought. I jerked the wheel to avoid getting hit and instinctively hit the brake. It was a good thing there was no one behind us and that we weren't going that fast. We skidded a bit and the engine stalled, but Daddy coached me calmly though getting the car started. Once I remembered to breathe, I could actually hear his instructions. We got rolling and up to speed just as the transition road was merging into the slow lane.

I was thankful for the short distance we had to travel to reach the Ganesha exit. I was still shaking when I made the left turn and glided down the hill past the high school and made the right into Sintown. Then I made the quick left into the driveway. When I had turned off the car, Clo spoke. "What did you learn today?" I stammered and tried to recount the steps to getting the car started after the stall. Daddy saw I was way off the mark, so he began at the beginning.

"You know I wouldn't have let you drive if I didn't think you were ready. You're good, but you need practice. And you need to learn your way around. Where you are will determine which road you take to get where you're going. You need to learn how to take care of a car—not just washing and gas, but tires, brakes, and oil too. You have to get used to paying for your car. You have to be ready for the unexpected. You can't *NOT* be prepared. Do you feel prepared to get your license?"

"I thought I was," I whispered.

When I graduated, and it was determined I would follow Sammy to Cal State Fullerton, Daddy decided I needed a car. Early in '71, he traded in the '65 for a brand-new, canary-yellow bug. I immediately adopted that car—high back seats, black interior, wider wheelbase. The car didn't have an air conditioner, but it did have an FM radio. Now I could get my jazz with Chuck Niles and others on KBCA-105.1 and my rock n' roll on KMET and KLOS. I still had to head to the AM band for R & B with KDAY and KGFJ, but I didn't care. One Saturday morning toward the end of June, Daddy and I went back to where he bought his yellow Bug in La Habra. The dealership was near Hughes, where he worked, and not very far from the Cal State Fullerton campus. When we walked into the showroom, none of the five salesmen lying in wait for customers approached us. It was left to Clo to ask if a particular salesman was there. A disinterested guy went and got the man Daddy was there to see.

When the second guy came out, Daddy shook his hand and introduced me. I nodded and tried to follow the conversation between them. Daddy asked about some percentage, and the salesman nodded. He led us into a small room with a glass wall, a particle-board desk, and three chairs. He asked us to sit. I looked out into the showroom and noticed that everyone was looking at Clo and me. Just like it was whenever Daddy did business in a place like this, we were the only Negroes for miles. The salesman opened a thick folder and handed Clo a pen.

He began explaining what had to be signed and where. Daddy signed and initialed where instructed until he got to the purchase price. When he spoke, his voice was dry and terse. "You told me the car had been discounted by 3 percent. But this is the original price." The salesman looked at my father and said his manager would not discount the price but would refund the 3 percent after the sale. Clo frowned. "That was not our agreement. I agreed to return to your dealership to buy a second car in six months if you would discount the purchase price of 3 percent. The salesman countered that the dollar amount would be the same and the sales manager had approved this arrangement. I was thoroughly confused.

Daddy stood up. The salesman looked at him and pursed his lips. He seemed genuinely unprepared for a colored guy to be speaking to him like this. He didn't understand why this mattered. He stammered and repeated that the dollar amount of the savings would be the same and tried to get Daddy to sit down. Daddy refused and said, "First of all, you promised me on the phone that this could be done and I took you at your word. Second, you want the higher purchase price on that chart in the manager's office so you can compete for top salesperson. Third, I want it on the record that I got this discount as a reward for my repeat business. If I can't have that, I might as well go to the dealer down the road. I can get the same car there."

The salesman asked Daddy to wait while he spoke to his manager. Less than five minutes later, he returned with a blank sales form. I doubted that he had talked to anybody. He began filling in the form with the new figures while Daddy and I watched. I glanced at Clo a few times just to see what I could see. His expression never changed. His eyes never left that form.

Once the form was finished, and all the papers were signed, we went out on the lot to see a 1971 Clementine Red Volkswagen Beetle waiting for us. I have to point out here that this was orange, not any kind of red. It was the orange-est car I had ever seen. I was like a kid on Christmas, but I knew my role was to mimic my father in attitude and demeanor. The salesman gave Daddy the keys but ignored Clo's extended hand. We watched him as he turned on his heel to walk away. When he had returned to the showroom, Daddy turned and gave me the keys.

"Follow me. I'll see you at home."

I essentially lived in my car. Between work at the Post Office, getting to class at Cal State Fullerton and just general running around, I was always in my car.

My orange '71 Bug was an expression of who I was. Just like my partner Jay did with his '69, I took the muffler off and installed a set of headers that gave the car a low growl instead of the normal pocket-full-of-change sound that came

My pride and joy. 1971 Clementine Red Volkswagen Beetle, aka Bug.

out of the puny air-cooled, four-stroke VW engine. We also took the regular rear tires off and replaced them with huge oversized tires on beautiful Cragar rims. We then discovered that our stock fenders were too small to accommodate the new tires. Those were soon switched out for battleship-grey, flared fiberglass fenders. We scraped many a knuckle working under those cars to replace those fenders. Bumpers had to be removed; taillights disconnected. Of course, everything had to be put back in place so that it actually worked. It wasn't very long before we knew we would have to replace the rear shocks to keep the new fenders off the oversized tires, but that would have to wait for more cash flow.

Inside the car, we dressed up our door knobs, radio controls, glove box, and gear shift with wood grain inserts and covers. Everybody had something dangling from their rearview. Mine was a rotating assortment of beads and afro-centric pendants and buttons. Jay and I both bought smaller racing-style steering wheels with a spongy neoprene covering. These "donuts" made the car a little harder to steer, but they were cool as hell.

What made my Bug mine was what played on the stereo. But before I talk about the music, we have to discuss the stereo itself. This was at a time when music and the way we listened to it changed in phenomenal ways. We had grown up on 45s and LPs on the Hi-Fi. Music was portable only on the radio, and you had to listen to what the deejay played, complete with commercials and idiots talking over the beginning and endings of our favorite songs. The more inventive of us tried to record music with a mic next to the speaker and two fingers poised over the play and record buttons.

Then came the 4-track tape player.

The under-dash mounted, 4-track tape player turned our cars into little concert halls on wheels. All of a sudden our favorite albums were on a cartridge that could be shoved into a player and enjoyed with pretty good sound quality. The 4-track was state of the art for a while, and I was the tape player and speaker installer for a bunch of our friends. I spent many an afternoon under dashboards and crawling around trunks to perfectly position speakers. I cut more holes in door panels than I care to mention.

Then came the 8-track player. The sound quality was much better with an 8-track because there was supposed to be twice as much musical information on the magnetic tape as before. We couldn't wait to switch out the tape players, but we were still beholden to the linear order of the songs as recorded on the original album. You could reverse the tape and play the song going in the other direction, but you would drop into the middle of a song, and it was a pain to rewind or fast-forward to the beginning. At one point, we found someone with an 8-track recorder who would custom-make tapes for us. The problem was that he charged more than we would pay for an album at the Wherehouse over on Indian Hill. And we had to supply the records.

And then came the cassette tape player.

When we saw the first cassette tape players for cars, what stood out was the built-in AM-FM receiver, so when we wanted to tune in to 105 or KLOS or KMET on the FM band or KGFJ, KJLH, KRLA or KHJ on the AM side, we could jam with the same fidelity we got off our recorded music. This was driven by the disc jockeys who played the music. These were guys (and they were mostly guys) who knew their music and their musicians. It was nothing for these dudes to play a cut we would never hear on AM radio that might last six or seven minutes. We ate it up.

Of course, the new-found flexibility of recording our music in any order we wanted turned us into deejays of a sort because the group of partners I ran with had very eclectic tastes. Especially Jay. One minute he'd be playing the Spinners or Rufus and the next be blasting Frank Zappa and the Mothers of Invention. We played the Stones and Led Zeppelin alongside

Aretha and Sly Stone, and we did it with the windows down. There was just no telling what we put on our cassettes. If I didn't have the album I needed, I could always get it from one of the fellas. I guess these would be called mixtapes now, and we juxtaposed artists and songs and themes. We even read reviews of the different brands of cassette tapes to make sure we got the most music possible out of our hardware.

I once asked Jay if he worried about what folks would think hearing rock 'n roll or Joni Mitchell coming out of his car. His response was blunt. "I don't care one way or the other. I like a lot of music, and I'm gonna listen to what I'm gonna listen to. I refuse to only listen to R&B, or only Jazz because that's what Black folks are supposed to listen to. Besides, the musicians don't seem to care 'cause they, play on each others' albums all the time."

The music we listened to opened a whole new perspective to popular culture, the movies we saw, and the magazines we read: Rolling Stone, Mother Jones, and National Lampoon commented on everything and anything, not just music. They were almost required reading 'cause we were going to either talk about some article or hear it referenced by someone on the radio. We took our music and the associated points of culture seriously. We also listened to sharp political satire by Mort Sahl, Dick Gregory, The Last Poets and Richard Pryor. KRLA-AM used to have a show, the Credibility Gap, that skewered just about everyone on a bipartisan basis. From LBJ to Tricky Dick, we listened religiously.

Music was a huge part of what our Bugs meant to us. Our cars represented approaching adulthood, responsibility, and mobility. Our music represented our understanding of the world around us. Weather Report fused jazz with R&B while Stevie explored different instruments. Jackson Browne and the Eagles told California stories, while we could always appreciate

EWF and TOP. All of this was built on an understanding of the giants like Bird, Trane, and Miles. We would get in our Bugs and travel far and wide to see concerts that ranged from Freddie Hubbard at the Light House in Hermosa Beach to Marvin Gaye at the Forum to Van Morrison at the Pasadena Civic. Jay and I once drove all the way to Santa Barbara to see Rick Wakeman and YES in concert. I guess the point is, we thought a lot about the intersection of our cars and our music. One meant freedom to go when and where we needed to go. The other meant we were going to enjoy the ride.

WHAT LAWN JOCKEY?

WE HAD JUST started our senior year at Ganesha. Ronald, Jay, and I had finished almost all of our high school requirements and were going to spend this year working, just marking time until graduation. I couldn't even tell you what pushed our behavior from smack-talking to indignation to rebellious action. It was one of those instances when youthful bravado just went way off the rails.

That Afro and T-shirt was pretty much my uniform back in the day.

We usually met up with each other around ten, after work to sit around playing Spades and talking trash. James and I had just arrived at his house on Hillside with burgers from Golden Ox. It was Ron's day off, and he had been waiting for us in James' driveway. Ron and I followed James into his room near the front of the house. When James turned on his stereo, Stevie's "Talking Book" album was playing. We finished the round of burgers, fries, and shakes and were feeling pretty good about ourselves. We were all sons of lower-middle-class Black families and constantly comparing notes about the similarities in our upbringing. James was originally from South Carolina, by way of Louisiana and Virginia and Catholic. I was from Chicago by way of St. Louis and Compton—Catholic. Ron was from Louisiana—Baptist. All three of us were working as box-boys at markets in town and had some change in our pockets.

The conversation was our normal stuff: girls, sports, girls, politics, girls, the fellas, girls, jobs, girls, meddling parents, girls, college, and girls. At some point, James mentioned a topic that he harped on from time to time: the house around the corner that had a black lawn jockey with exaggerated, obnoxious red lips in the front yard. This jockey was a constant irritant to him, and he swore he was going to do something about it someday. Even though we agreed with him in principle, Ron and I just laughed it off. We'd heard this song before.

At this point, I have to provide some context. James, Ron and I were part of an eclectic group of Black students at school. Our families were pioneers of a sort, having moved to a suburb twenty-five miles east of L.A. where the streets were wide and clean, the schools were pretty good, and things were okay in the late 60s and early 70s. We had the benefit of honors and advanced classes, and the Black Studies courses we had demanded were coming into their own. While reading DuBois, Douglass, Wright, Hurston, and Washington, we were watching the social upheaval occurring all around us. Civil Rights victories were being won at the same time marchers and Panthers were being beaten and killed. We realized that the world we were about to graduate into was a damn sight different from the one our parents had known. We had disdain for our parents for pursuing a middle-class life, and we were oblivious to the tangible advantages they provided us. We derisively called our mothers "Martha Middle-Class" while enjoying the fruits of their very real labor as teachers, nurses, and mid-level managers.

In our group, affectionately referred to as "The Fellas" even with the large contingent of female members, we were painfully aware that our exhortations of "Black is Beautiful" stood alongside vestiges of our history. One vestige of this history showed images of African Americans who reminded us of the "bad ole days" when we were portrayed as big-lipped, slow-walking, dim-witted, subservient cretins. Enter the Lawn Jockey.

As we talked, James got more and more riled up. Ron and I didn't help; we were goading him and saying that he was all talk and no action. He got a determined look on his face, which indicated now was the time for us to strike a blow against a clearly racist and demeaning characterization. Ron and I didn't disagree with him; we just weren't feeling the call to action. I shuffled the cards and looked to my right for Ronald to cut the cards. Without even looking, he tapped the deck, signifying that he was cool with the shuffle.

James would not let it go. He claimed that if we were not willing to get rid of that damn lawn jockey, then we were complicit—by default, of approving the jockey's presence— and had no right to complain about it. Indeed, he accused US of being all talk and no fight because we wouldn't join him in striking a blow for liberation. At some point, we succumbed to the argument and started asking procedural questions, like:

When? How? Ronald looked over the tops of his wire-rimmed glasses and smiled at James. He still thought this misguided adventure could be averted.

It seems James had put a lot of thought into this. Not necessarily quality thought, just thought. "NOW! We can use my car. We'll throw it in the trunk and then throw it in the wash." For the uninformed, "the wash" was the system of drainage canals that snaked through town. It was maybe thirty feet deep and twenty feet wide, built to handle the run-off from the periodic heavy rains and flash floods that came to our desert landscape in the winter.

Anyway, we all started signifyin' and whoopin' and cussin' that damn lawn jockey and the people who owned the house where it stood. Before we knew it, we had put our cards face-down on the table and were in the Mustang, off down the street—quietly, of course. But how quiet can you be in a '65 Mustang? We decided turning off the lights would have to suffice. It dawned on each one of us at the same time that we were now committed to this course of action and couldn't back out without major face-losing. We all fell silent as we crept along. Thinking back on it, we must have looked pretty silly sitting three deep in a muscle car, rollin' through suburbia, scoping out a lawn jockey.

We all saw it at the same time. We stopped down the street, on the other side. As we cased our objective, we talked about various ways to pull this off. We argued about how to get the car as close as possible to shorten the distance we would have to carry it. It stood maybe ten feet in from the corner of the property where the driveway met the sidewalk. The lawn and driveway of the house had a slope, but for some reason that didn't register with any of us. I don't remember coming to a consensus about our plan of attack. At some point, we just started in. Jay moved the car closer and turned around to back up into the driveway. He shut off the engine, and the car drifted back quietly. When it hit the dip at the bottom of the driveway, it lost all its momentum and started rocking back and forth. Ronald told him to start the engine and try to back up the driveway again. Jay said that would just attract attention and besides, we were wasting time. "Just get out and get it!" James snapped. I answered that this was all his idea, and now Ronald and I were doing all the work?

Meanwhile, Ronald had skulked up to the jockey and grabbed it. James and I saw him jerk at the statue and that it didn't move. We ran up and instantly understood that a three-foot, cast-iron statue on a cement base is extremely heavy. Aware that if we were going to take the thing, we had to do it now, we grabbed different parts and surprised ourselves by actually moving it. But carrying it was another story.

We put it down and scoped how far it was to the car. Someone counted to three, and we hoisted and started hauling it in tiny baby steps. Then we started tipping downhill and couldn't stop. Ronald let go, and James and I couldn't hold our parts, so the jockey fell to the cement and tumbled to the bottom of the driveway, clanging like the Liberty Bell. We all hit the ground and froze. I, for one, was ready to call it a night. But James got the keys and popped the trunk while Ron ran back to the statue. They tried to hoist it into the ass end of the car, a good four feet off the ground. Reluctantly, I got under it, and we managed to get that sucker over the lip of the trunk. The joy at our display of testosterone was instantly shattered when the jockey clanged even louder in the well of the trunk. I fully expected police at any second. Jay slammed the trunk while Ronald and I piled in. James started the car and gunned the engine. When he put it into gear, the car shot forward, tumbling Ronald into the back seat. The car fishtailed to the left and then right as Jay tried to correct his steering.

James got us out of the neighborhood and merged into traffic on one of the main drags. He drove around, turning randomly, constantly looking in his rear views. I asked him where he was going, and we knew right away that he had not visualized himself actually throwing the jockey into a specific wash, just *a* wash. Ronald told James to stop the car and decide where we were going to ditch it. We all started calling out places where we could get it out of the trunk and into the wash without being seen. We considered taking it over to the South Side just to move out of our part of town. After a couple rounds of stupid suggestions, we decided to go over to the back of Kennedy Park. It made sense because we could roll to the back, hidden from view, and finish this. What we hadn't expected was the car that was parked back there, lights off and windows all steamed up. James was about to turn around and leave when the driver of the other car must've thought he and his friend were busted because he tore outta there quick, fast and in a hurry. James cut the lights and backed up to the chain-link fence on the edge of the wash. We all jumped out, and once James opened the trunk, started grabbing at the thing, trying to get it out of the well. We managed to get it up on the lip, but then we all turned and looked. We would have to lift it another two feet to get it over the chain-link.

But we figured we had come this far; it was not going to stop us. Ronald and I were on the base end, and James was on the head and shoulders end. We counted to three and clean-jerked that sucker off the car and over the fence. We thought it had cleared and was on its way into the wash when we noticed the jockey's outstretched hand caught in the chain link. For what seemed an eternity, those grinning red lips and bug eyes stared at us like someone refusing to say goodbye. James couldn't believe that after everything else, the evidence of our misadventure would be hanging on the fence. He swooped around with his foot and kicked. The jockey lost his grip and fell. The crash at the bottom of the wash was dull and gritty. Unbelievably, the cement of the base hitting the cement of the wash left it standing upright, even if a little tipsy. Occasionally, I think about the muddy flash-flood waters seasonally washing past that lawn jockey, debris and garbage catching on its edges. We didn't stay there looking very long.

James got in the car and started it, but didn't gun the engine. When Ronald and I were in, he pulled away slowly and drove calmly back to his house. He found an O'Jays tape and let it play. Jay was singing along and chair-dancin'. We passed the former home of the stolen jockey before heading down Ronald's street. We all grinned and looked straight ahead. When we got back to Jay's house, we all sat down and picked up our cards. Jay started "What's Going On?" Ronald won the bid and picked up the kitty. After a minute or so, he tossed all of his cards down and looked at James and me. He didn't say anything and just sat there with this benign grin on his face. I looked at him and then at James with a wordless "Hell, Yes!" look. James just looked at us with a kind of appreciation for a couple of friends.

That adventure has stayed with me. What it symbolized in 1970 lives on in modern-day caricatures that continue to demean and insult Black folks. What Ronald, James, and I shared that evening has also stayed with me. However silly and pointless the trashing of a simple cast-iron icon of racism might have been, I can't forget the rush of meeting a challenge and rising to an occasion, however odd. We still bust up about that night, but we have also been contemplative. That lawn jockey would not be the last spitefully derogatory image I would encounter in my life, and I have always been silently proud that we resisted that despicable imagery from day one.

SAMMY'S SWEATER

THE HOUSE WE lived in on Avalon was the shape of a shoebox, just like every other tract house in Sintown. It was a wood frame structure on a cement slab with drywall and cheap aluminum sliding windows. You could lock the doors and block the windows from sliding too far open, but the house just wasn't that secure.

Sammy's Sweater, lower right.

During my junior year, our house burgularized three or four times. They took stereos, cameras, leather jackets, and other stuff that could be quickly fenced and turned into cash. Each time, Momma and Daddy would report the theft to the insurance company, and our losses would be replaced. Then just as soon as we would replace the things, we would get hit again. Sadly, the Pomona PD had not a clue as to who was doing this. At least that's what they told us.

Our sense of violation and frustration came to a head when Daddy devised a barrier gate across the front door and windows that would seal the perimeter and make it harder to get into the house. Eight feet tall, 2 x 6 framing, 1 x 4 slats set every 3 inches at a 45-degree angle with big hinges and hardware. Glitches and the idiosyncrasies of the house caused head scratching and adjustments, but we got that sucker built to his specs. It didn't help. We got hit again. Again Daddy submitted a claim. Again we received new merchandise to replace the stolen. Again the Pomona PD scratched their heads. That's when I saw Sammy's sweater.

On an otherwise regular day, I was walking down the corridor at school, coming from the theater & music department on the north end of the campus and going toward the science wing near the front courtyard. I wasn't paying much attention to anything until I saw Jerry Suggs. It wasn't so much that I saw Jerry as it was that I saw the baby-blue and white, cable-knit, short-sleeve ski sweater he was wearing. A sweater just like it, belonging to Sammy, had been stolen in burglary #2. When I saw what I knew was Sammy's sweater on Jerry, I thought about confronting him and asking where he got it. That thought lasted about a nanosecond because, although he wasn't any taller than me, Jerry had biceps on his biceps. He could have and would have beaten the snot out of me in his sleep. I remember trying to tackle him in during a one-on-one drill when we were both on the "B" football team. He had put a knee and thigh in my chest and blown all of the breath out of my body, and I had not deterred him in any way. It would not have taken a lot of provocation for him to dispatch me to the nurse's office if he felt I was a threat. Discretion being the better part of valor, I quickly made a left into the main office. I told Mrs. Robinson in the attendance office that I needed to talk to the Assistant Principal. I went to Mrs. Robinson because she looked after kids in a way that I appreciate to this day. Her husband worked security out in the parking lot and her kids, Deanna and Ricky, were classmates and friends. I even went steady with Deanna for about three weeks while we were at Marshall Jr. High.

Mrs. Robinson listened to my shorthand description of the sweater incident and got me in to see Mr. Evans. He seemed uninterested in what I was saying until I got to the part where I said, "I think Jerry broke into my house and stole my brother's sweater." At that point, he called the Pomona PD and had me sit in his office until they came. After I talked to them for what seemed like a long time, they summoned Jerry to the counseling office. Mr. Evans' secretary tried to get ahold of Jerry's parents but to no avail. I understand they talked to Jerry for about ten minutes and then cuffed him and took him to the police station. At that point, Mr. Evans told me to go on to class; he seemed unconcerned about any repercussions my actions might trigger. I'd been hoping for a high school version of a witness-protection program. No such luck.

Over the next few days, the Ganesha Grapevine was alive with rumors that a huge Sintown burglary ring had been busted. An abandoned house on Canterbury had been used as a warehouse for stolen goods collected from break-ins all over the Westside. Speakers, stereos, car stereos, amplifiers, tape decks, TV's, jewelry, watches and the like. This house was like Black Market Central.

Jerry was only one of a ring of guys who would case houses

and wait for adults to go to work and kids to go to school before they struck. They even had it timed out so they would go back to houses they had hit previously once they thought the insurance money had come in. Momma was afraid that since I had fingered Jerry with Sammy's sweater, I might be targeted somehow for payback. I told her not to worry 'cause I had spoken to Mr. Evans, and nothing bad had happened the day I reported the incident. I told her I didn't think anybody even knew I had identified him, so she shouldn't worry. I did look over my shoulder for a few days but soon forgot about Jerry and the ring of thieves.

A couple of months later, one of the Pomona PD detectives called Momma and told her young Mister Suggs had a hearing scheduled and that I could attend if I wanted to. The officer said I wouldn't have to testify because it was a hearing, not a trial. He thought me being there could provide a certain amount of closure for our family. Momma was adamant: I wasn't going anywhere near that hearing room. Daddy was non-committal; he wanted me to make the decision. Did I want to see the hearing? What would it do for me to see this guy get what was coming to him? Was I afraid of him, or his friends and family, seeing me there?

In the end, I decided to attend the hearing. Momma was furious. Daddy told me to be careful. When I got to the courthouse, I was surprised that this was decidedly not Perry Mason. The court and the personnel were a lot more informal than I had imagined. Jerry was not present, and there were only a few people in the hearing room. I sat in the back row for spectators, all the way to the left side of the room. There was a dark, weary-looking woman sitting in the first row, all the way to the right. She kinda looked like Jerry, but I couldn't tell from my vantage point and I didn't want to stare. From the side, she had a stoic look frozen on her face and stared straight ahead. Her dreary familiarity with the surroundings suggested she had been through this before.

Suddenly, all sorts of activity occurred. A bailiff escorted Jerry into the hearing room and sat him down next to his lawyer or advocate. A court-reporter was at her little machine and ready in a matter of seconds. Another lawyerly looking man sifted through some papers and exhaled. The hearing officer came in and sat where I expected to see a judge. He called the hearing to order, and things started happening very fast. The lawyer/advocates identified themselves, and Jerry was asked to identify himself. There was a bunch of legalese spoken among the participants, and I didn't understand a word of it. With his head down, I couldn't see Jerry's face so I couldn't gauge his reaction to the proceedings. From where I was sitting, all I could see was the back of his head. The woman in the front row never betrayed any response or reaction.

When everyone rose to their feet, I knew there was something important about to happen. The hearing officer asked Jerry if he understood why everyone was there that day. He said quietly that he did. The hearing officer continued without even acknowledging Jerry's response. He explained that this wasn't Jerry's first contact with the juvenile system and that the evidence against him and his statements left the hearing officer no choice but to send Jerry to a juvenile camp in the desert until his twenty-first birthday. I figured Jerry was maybe 16 or 17, so this could be four years—anyway, it was gonna' be for a while.

The hearing wasn't about guilt or innocence. That had already been established. It was simply to decide what was to be done with Jerry. Strangely, as I watched what was going on, I felt a little bad for him. Although he could be hard at times, he was cool. I had known of him, even if I didn't know him well, going back to Marshall. And, after all, he was a son of Sintown.

As I understood it through the Grapevine, two or three other high school dudes just like Jerry were being sent away for all these thefts, but it didn't appear that whoever was running the show was being held accountable. And even though Jerry and his friends had ripped my family off more than once, the punishment didn't seem to fit the crime.

I sat there watching Jerry as the lawyer/advocates and the hearing officer gathered up their things and exited the room. The bailiff started to take Jerry back from where he had brought him. He paused for a second so Jerry could speak to the stoic woman, but their contact amounted to a brief squeeze of his hand in hers. Jerry's head turned slightly, and I'm pretty sure he saw me in the far corner. I'm not sure he even knew who I was; there was no sign of recognition. I feel almost certain he never made the connection between Sammy's sweater and his current circumstance.

The rest of the details about that event that have faded. I had to get to work right after the hearing, so I let go of the experience almost as soon as I walked out of the courthouse. It was a bigger deal to Momma and Daddy than it was to me. But what I haven't forgotten was seeing my brother's sweater walking toward me. That image represented the divergence of our lives; Jerry and me. I was stumbling toward college and a new chapter of opportunity. Jerry was on his way to Juvie. As a parent, I have tried to give my kids an appreciation for blessings and circumstances. Do the best you can where you are with what you have. Not an original thought, but one that has served me well over the years.

HELEN SNODGRASS

WHEN WE ENTERED Ganesha High School in the fall of 1968, the "Fellas" were a cross section of the Sintown community. Not all of the Fellas were boys and we didn't even think of ourselves as "The Fellas". There were Fellas who came in later and some that left earlier, as in all high schools. We ran the gamut: honor students, class clowns, average students, athletes, musicians, singers, shop whizzes, cheerleaders and science squares. I guess you could call the core of the Fellas James, Ronald, Malcolm, Freddie, Joyce, Debra, Orson, Eborah, Chuckie,

Some of the Fellas: 'Bout to Graduate!

Keith, Willie, Reggie, La Blanche, Cheryl, Ralph, Corliss and a few more.

There was a subsection of us who were listening to the news and taking note of the events that were bombarding us on a daily basis. By the fall of our 10th grade year, the U.S.S. Pueblo had been seized by North Korea; The Viet Cong had launched the Tet Offensive; President Johnson had declined to run for re-election; Dr. King and another Kennedy had been gunned down; Poor people had marched on Washington; and, there were riots at the National Democratic Convention. That was just in the first nine months of 1968. Our parents and families were discussing and debating the various facets of the Civil Rights Movement and the Viet Nam War. We had seen our fathers and brothers and uncles and cousins being swept up in the draft. Assassinations had peppered our childhoods and adolescent years: John Kennedy, Malcolm X and Medgar Evers had preceded King and Kennedy. In my family, it was open warfare between my oldest brothers and one of them even called our father an Uncle Tom because he worked for a defense contractor.

The Fellas were being exposed to the classic books of great Black writers by some of our older brothers and sisters as they handed them down to us through their college classes. There was an orchestrated crusade afoot to discredit and destroy our Black leaders as Nixon barked "LAW and ORDER" all during the '68 campaign and began to implement his "Southern Strategy." When Johnson refused to stand for re-election and Kennedy was killed, the Democrats were left with a tearful McCarthy and a bland Vice President Humphrey after the riotous convention in Chicago.

Tommie Smith and John Carlos would raise their fists

in Mexico City after some Black athletes boycotted the '68 Olympic that fall. Some of us had parents that had attended historically black colleges like Lincoln (in Philly and Jeff City, Missouri), Howard, Norfolk State, Grambling, Southern and Winston Salem. We were watching the exploits of Earl Monroe, Walt "Clyde" Frazier and Jim Brown. Motown and Stax were our soundtracks along with an inkling of jazz and funk influences. Add to this mix big, rampant conversations about drugs, free love and rock 'n roll.

So when we walked onto the Ganesha campus as sophomores, the Fellas were expecting something from high school. We just didn't know what that something was. All of us were more-than-capable students and "readin', writin' and 'rithmatic" were not going to cut it. I ran for sophomore class president and won then didn't have what you could call an agenda. I knew I really wasn't interested in the purely social calendar the student council had on the table. I got to approve the class ring design that had already been ordered and escort the sophomore class princess to the Christmas formal. I think the word I'm looking for is, "ceremonial."

At the same time, many of the Fellas were taking advanced/honors classes in math, science, history and English. The first two subjects we struggled through hating certain teachers and enjoying others. The last two had content that ran directly counter to what we knew to be true. Some of us had ancestors that were slaves and parents who had grown up in segregation before escaping various southern and midwestern states. The historical tales we were being told in regular U.S. History courses completely excised us from the American story. Myths about our country's founding neglected to mention the free slave labor that fueled the expansion of the Grand Experiment.

Even worse, the literature we were assigned to read for our classes had nothing to do with the reality that the Fellas were talking about every day. Where was anything from the Harlem Renaissance or the new civil rights authors like James Baldwin? Don't get me wrong. We were completely ignorant of the breadth and depth of Black History or the canon of Black literature. But in my house, alongside Poe, Twain and a host of other American writers, we read Woodson, Washington and Bu Bois. We read *EBONY* and *JET* before we read *LIFE, LOOK* or the *SATURDAY EVENING POST* magazines. We read the episodic historical writings of Lerone Bennet in Ebony and were aware of people like Carver and Bethune and places like Grambling, Southern and Howard Universities. In fact, the fellas came from families that knew all of the American myths as well as the American reality that undergirded that mythology. Jim Crow was a real person to us.

Building up to election day in November, 1968 people all over Pomona supported Dr. James Bell for School Board and he became the first Black member of that body at the same time the country was electing Richard Nixon as president. Part of Dr. Bell's platform was that our high school classes would have more representative content and that Black and Latino students would have more access to advanced/honors classes than they had in the past. Given the traditional stance of everything about Ganesha and the other schools in Pomona, this was no easy proposal to accept or execute. Many folks suspected the schools wouldn't make these changes even if so directed by the school board.

When the school board did indeed approve limited changes to the curriculum to offer classes in African American History and African American Literature, the high school administrators, almost in unison, declared, "we don't have anyone on staff qualified to develop syllabi and outlines for these classes." This was not a dodge or an excuse. It was the truth. As educated and erudite as our English and social studies teachers might have been, they were clueless on how to present Black American contributions that had been all but ignored within the curriculum. They had not been taught this material in their history and literature classes, from kindergarten through graduate school, so they could not teach it.

Then Helen Schneider stepped up before our junior year. Miz Schneider was a slight little woman, devoutly Catholic by upbringing in Iowa. Freddie called her Miz Snodgrass after a white, waif-looking actress of the day, Carrie Snodgrass. Freddie always gave people nicknames, especially those he cared about, and Miz Schneider had gone to bat for any number of students including Freddie and his brother, Ron, when their home situations warranted a change of scenery. Both lived with her and her husband, Gar and their kids at different times.

When she decided to teach the literature class, she also realized she knew less than nothing about the subject. But she had friends and colleagues at the Claremont Colleges who gave her a crash course in Black authors and books and the history and culture that produced them. She spent the entire summer before our junior year consuming and dissecting the books, essays and poems she would guide us through. We later found out that during that first year, she had consumed a ton of books and writings that were brand new to her and that she was reading some of the pieces just a few chapters ahead of the assignments she was giving us.

More important than the specific books and authors she introduced us to, was the questioning and discussion and debate she demanded we use in her class. We examined books and writers we were seeing for the first time. She helped us navigate the discomfort we felt at confronting this material. Topics, dialects, situations and issues were introduced and debated, but with care. Many of us had an immature anger about the degradation of our ancestors, even as we enjoyed the benefits of their struggles. Somehow, Miz Schneider tempered our ire with more celebratory examples of poetry, prose and music that we dug as we discovered Ellington, BeBop and Rhythm & Blues. There were discussions that first introduced us to the voice of a slave woman. We talked about the role of the Black athlete and the Black politician. Pioneers and trailblazers were discovered and debated. All this from a woman who was running just ahead of us as she learned what she wanted to teach us.

While we debated and questioned each other, the contradiction of a slight white woman teaching our history and literature was not lost on us. We didn't hold what she was against her because who she was is the more important aspect of this situation. Miz Schneider saw an instructional void that no one else was stepping forward to fill. Honestly, I can't think of anyone on that campus who would have bought as much passion to teaching such an unruly bunch of wanna-be scholars as she did. She gave as good as she got when we challenged her with questions and opinions. She did not flinch in arguing for peaceful, nonviolent change even as we were seeing lynchings, assassinations and war all around us. Although she knew there were times when war and violence was a reluctant course of action, she cited countless Black Americans like Douglass, King and Marshall as examples of men who made the case through oratory and legal action. One lesson learned in Miz Schneider's classes was that in most instances, victory was going to be a long time coming and if you are going to fight for justice, you must be in the fight for the long haul.

The Fellas are older now and we have each made our way. We've married, raised kids, seen grandkids and built careers. The roots of our activism and our understanding of the world flow through that class. Aside from my almost complete dedication to the Ganesha theater department, I don't remember a whole lot of classes and even fewer teachers. Show me a yearbook and I'll recall a few details. But the class that impacted me then and now was that one taught by Miz Helen Snodgrass.

CLO THE PUNISHER

DISCIPLINE IN DADDY'S house was an adventure. He was barely 5'11" and really soft-spoken. He wasn't going to physically intimidate anybody, and yelling was not his style. So teaching a lesson required stern thought and consideration.

It was a Friday night in the spring of my senior year, and we (me and my girlfriend, Laura) were double-dating with Eric and his girlfriend. I was going to drive Daddy's '65 beige VW over to Eric's, and then we would take off in his car to get the girls. When I got to his house, he was finishing the detail on his car and drinking a tall can of Olde English 800 Malt Liquor. He offered me a sip, and I took it. For those who don't know, Olde English 800 is some nasty stuff. I had to struggle that crap down my throat. Made you wonder what the first 799 formulae were like. The after-taste was bitter and disgusting. So I took two more sips.

We got in Eric's '67 Mustang and turned the cassette

of the Stones "Tumbling Dice" up to barely bearable levels. Conversation was impossible, but that didn't stop us from trying. The booze was kicking in. Eric's girlfriend, Marie, got in the front and I got in the back. Laura sat next to me.

If you've ever been in the back seat of a Mustang, you know it's cramped. Eric had, lifted the rear end of his car to accommodate the over-sized tires that he loved to peel out. With the stiff, heavy-duty shock absorbers he had installed, Laura and I felt like we were falling forward the entire night and endured every bleeping bump and crack in the road. Then the vodka and orange juice appeared.

I don't remember much besides singing the Stones "Brown Sugar" at the top of my lungs and puking my guts out. Richard Pryor had a line in one of his routines, "I ain't got nothin' left to throw up but my nuts." That was me. I needed to lie down. I needed to be still. When I realized we were headed back to Eric's house, it dawned on me that I still had to drive Daddy's car home. A challenge, but I insisted I could handle it. It wasn't that far. I wasn't that dizzy. I could drive in between the waves of nausea, and of course, I could drive in first 'cause I certainly wasn't getting that VW into any other gear. But Somehow, it was decided that Laura would drive the VW to my house with me in the passenger seat. Eric would follow her and then take her home. I didn't contribute to the decision, but I felt pretty good about it. Because even though I had been drinking, riding around Pomona till two in the morning, and embarrassing myself by barfing, at least I would get the car home safely. Yeah.

As I negotiated the security gate, I figured I could get in the front door, quietly, then make a quick right through my bathroom and I could mercifully collapse into my bed. I could hear my bed calling me. I was mere yards away. My mind was already there. I could feel the pillow encase my head. Then I heard it.

"Jacques. Come here."

I followed the voice, bumping my way against the hallway walls to come into the living room. Daddy sat in his black naugahyde recliner. He was in his pajamas and a blue-green plaid flannel bathrobe. I remember thinking how well dressed Daddy looked. No wrinkles and everything smoothed out. The belt to his robe was tied around his waist with the ends perfectly laid out in his lap. He wasn't wearing his glasses, so his brow overshadowed his eyes. This only intensified the glare he already had focused on me.

"Where have you been?"

I thought it was a fair question. In my state, I was thankful that Pops was not a screamer. Later I would realize that having him yell at me might have been the easier course. But he calmly peppered me with questions about did I know what time it was and where had we been and what had I been drinking. I never did answer those questions, but it was not for lack of trying. My head was spinning and pounding. The nausea waves were coming back at shorter intervals. I managed to ask him if I could sit down. He said, "No." I had to stand there with zero equilibrium while he lectured and tried to get me to talk. And then he asked THE question.

"How did you get the car home?"

I was ready for this one. I knew Daddy would be impressed that I was looking out for him and taking care of his car by not driving it. "Laura drove it," I mumbled it. But I was proud. "WHAT? You let someone else drive my car? Does she have a license? Is she insured? Was she in the same condition as you?" I was amazed at how little I could actually tell him. Daddy was clearly not impressed with my decision making.

After a few minutes that felt like hours, Daddy let me go to bed. I remember thinking I had dodged a bullet. That lecture wasn't so bad. I'll probably be grounded for a while, and I won't be able to use cars, but I get to sleep now. I gobbled some undetermined number of aspirin and dropped onto the bed. I had recently taken my mattress out of its bunk-bed frame and put it directly on the floor, so it was a freefall. I fell asleep wondering how I could stop the room from spinning like a gyroscope.

It seemed like only a moment had passed when my head snapped up to an unbelievable racket. The room was still spinning and the sun was so bright it seared my eyes. It felt like someone had stuffed a big wad of cotton in my mouth. And I had to pee. That's when I discovered that I had given up trying to take my pants off because my brain didn't get the memo about taking off my shoes first. My shirt smelled like vomit, and I had no clue where my glasses were.

Now, my bedroom was in the front of the house, situated between the bathroom and the kitchen. Normally, I enjoyed being able to eavesdrop on conversations in the kitchen. Today, not so much. Daddy was cooking Saturday breakfast, and he was making sure I knew it. First with the pots and pans. He introduced every pot to every pan that morning. Nothing was set down on a counter gently. Every cabinet door and drawer was not just closed—it was slammed.

Then the welcome aromas of coffee, bacon, and fried potatoes began wafting into my room. I reveled in it for the first five seconds until the nausea started fighting back. I sat upright and tried to run into the bathroom, but my tangle of pants tackled me and slammed my swollen head into the closet door. I crawled the last few feet and got to the toilet bowl in time to dry heave the last little bit of bile in my stomach. I then managed to sit on the toilet and pee. That's when Daddy knocked hard and loud on my door and said, "Breakfast is ready!"

I pulled up my pants. Buttoning and zipping were optional at this point. I stumbled into the kitchen and slid into the breakfast nook bench seat. I longed for the support a normal chair would have given me and slumped with my head back against the upholstered nook. Daddy clanked a plate and silverware in front of me: Three greasy strips of bacon, two runny, sunny-side-up eggs, a ridiculously big mound of hash browns, and a dry piece of toast that dared me to eat it. The glass of orange juice he clunked on the table openly mocked me.

Daddy took a plate into Momma and let her eat breakfast in bed. I could hear him coo at her and say sweet things like, "Wake up, Sleepyhead." and "Rise and shine." He soon returned to the kitchen, fixed his plate and sat down at the table. He unfolded his LA Times to the editorial pages and checked out the Conrad cartoon. He chuckled and dug into his food.

I don't know who I was trying to impress, but I picked up my fork and cut into the egg. I must have nicked the yolk because the yellow stuff came gushing out. The translucence of the egg white and the barely cooked egg yolk brought back the waves. I tried to stifle the gag with a triangle of toast but that just quadrupled the cotton-mouth syndrome. The potatoes looked promising, but I soon discovered Daddy had cooked them without onions and with not a lick of seasoning. Straight up starch, blackened. I picked up a limp piece of bacon and saw the grease had coagulated on it except for this one little glop that ran off and plopped onto the plate.

Daddy didn't say a word. I didn't have the nerve to look at him, but I know he was watching me. He watched me suffer injury I had inflicted on myself. But, I think the worst pain I felt was knowing that I had let him down. Worse than the headache and nausea. Worse than the dizziness and the sensitivity to light, sound, smell, and temperature. I had not lived up to his expectations. He let me go back to bed after I vainly struggled to eat a few mouthfuls of food. Either that or he got sick of hearing me gag and moan. He let me sleep only till about noon. After all, it was Saturday, and there were chores to be done.

THE FIVE SISTERS

IN THE EARLY part of the twentieth century, Van Edward and Sarah Maude Perkins had five daughters: Juanita, Bernice, Jesse, Vanetta, and Sarah Louise. These five women were fiercely loyal to one another, and each answered to the name, "Sister," no matter who used it to address another. They produced eighteen grandchildren, all equally loyal to the name "Perkins." They were educators, executives, and activists. All of them married. Jesse died very young from asthma, leaving her husband Andy, with three kids. These Five Sisters are the cornerstone upon which our Perkins extended family rests. Their offspring, sometimes separated by time and distance, share experiences at the center of the universe, Grandma and Grandpa Perkins' house on North Market. St. Louis summer days, Big Breakfasts, holiday meals, and many other repasts all transpired within the walls of that house. These occasions were populated by the five sisters and their husbands and children. So 'cousin' isn't just an identifier in our family. To be a Perkins is to know strong black women at a time when their professional prospects led them to only teaching or nursing. They were funny, emotional, and absolutely dedicated to making sure Grandma and Grandpa had what they needed. Momma and Daddy had moved to Chicago, and Jesse died around 1951. Juanita, Vanetta, and Sarah Louise all stayed in St. Louis. Including their households and the house on North Market, these homes were all in the Villle. The Perkins family in St. Louis was a small, early social network where news traveled fast.

Fast forward more than five decades. I am putting on my socks and shoes the other day, and I noticed the small, faded, 58-year-old spot on the instep of my left foot. I touch it and remember how I got that scar.

Back in the day, whenever we visited St. Louis from Chicago, our first stop was always the house on North Market. Grandma and Grandpa had to be the first to know Bernice and her family were in town. She was married to Clovis, the scientist, and our arrival spread through the Perkins family grapevine instantly. Because we usually got there around midnight, Daddy could see his mother the next day. Momma had to see Grandma before either one of them went to sleep. But we kids wanted to bust loose. Our choices included sleeping at North Market, which would be good for the first night, or Wabada, Maffitt, and Red Bud. These place names represented the homes of Juanita, Vanessa, and Sarah Louise, respectively. We could also go over and stay with Daddy's mother, Elizabeth Burris Bordeaux Smith. Now we all loved Grandma Smith, but we didn't want to spend our whole vacation with her. Sammy, Jude, and Visey went over to Aunt Juanita and Uncle Ivan's house on Wabada or stayed at Grandma Perkins' on North

Market with our cousins Carolyn and Sara, Jesse's daughters. There were cousins of their age at both places, so three of the Bordeaux boys crashed wherever there was room. That left me to decide where to bunk. Since I didn't want to be anywhere near my brothers, I could invade Sarah and Jackie's house on Red Bud and listen to all the latest jams with cousins Denise and John. Or I could go to the Cartwright's house on Maffit; it had Raymond and Vanetta and their five children: Ramon, Greg, Tony, Cindy, and Angie. The original Bebe's Kids. The Wildest Bunch. Well, I decided to go over to Vanetta's. The truth is, I didn't so much decide to go over there; it was more like I decided to let the force of nature that was our Aunt Vanetta sweep me in whatever direction she was going.

The Cartwright "chirren" were a wonder to behold. All energy and argument. The one constant I remember from every visit to any Cartwright home, was the sound. Not noise— SOUND. Music, telephone conversations, the TV, the radio, and every other kind of sound that seven larger-than-life personalities squeezed into a confined space could make—all at the same time

I didn't fit in with the cacophony even though I was so often drawn to it. I was a quiet little cousin from Chicago. That household was a perpetual-motion traveling circus. If you got tired of watching one set of siblings going at it, just go into another room, and there were Ramon, Greg, and Tony with a two-on-one fast break in an imaginary game for the championship of bedroom basketball, using a bunch of rolled up socks as a ball. Greg called a foul and Ramon told him not to bring that weak s*** in here. All in a 10 x 10 bedroom. A musical score beneath all this action was provided by Uncle Ray and his Wall of Music. This is not an exaggeration or metaphor. The man had industrial metal shelving from floor to ceiling holding classic vintage pre-amps, amps, tuners, turntables, equalizers, and other things I can't even name. The real treasure was the vinyl. Records, records, and mo' records. Dizzy, Miles, Monk, Bird, Basie, Ellington, Sarah, Nina, Ella, Billie, and Dinah. All played VERY loud. Our entire family and most of western Missouri would defer to any Cartwright in their knowledge of music: Jazz in all of its incarnations, Be-Bop, R&B, Fusion, and so many more genres. Ramon was so serious about his musical heritage that he named his sons Miles and Parker in honor of Miles Davis and Charlie Parker. Further, any visit to a Cartwright home meant you were gonna hear some music you'd never heard before, and you were gonna hear it loud. The astounding thing was after a momentary bout of aural shock, you acclimated to the sound and didn't even try to have a conversation.

Anyway, back to the scar. One day while I was there, Raymond and Vanetta went off to work. They left all us kids at home. In my memory, this house was huge. It actually had two units, and I believe Raymond's mother lived in the other one. It was a red-brick, two story brownstone with a basement: Lots of room and lots of character. Like all the homes our scattered family inhabited in St. Louis, this one was old and dilapidated; ours after many waves of immigrant ownership. Like Daddy used to say, "These houses were decrepit by the time colored folks could buy them. Whites, Jews, Italians, and Germans were here before us. We're lucky they were still standing by the time we got them."

Rickety or not, these houses were our pieces of the rock. There was a tradition of home-ownership in our families. When we went "over so-and-so's house," we were going to a house. Very few of our relatives lived in apartments. The house on Maffit, in particular, had plenty of character. It needed some repair, but no more than most of the houses in the neighborhood. It had plenty of nooks and crannies—lots of places to hide in during Hide and Go Seek. That's where the scar comes in.

After a couple of rounds where the older boys (me, Ramon, and Greg) had a turn at seeking, it was Tony's turn to count. Now, I was playing on the Cartwright home court, and they knew—and took—all the good hiding spots. I had to use some imagination and skill to find a place where Tony wouldn't find me. I had been scoping out where people had been and thought I'd gotten the ideal spot. After everybody had caught their breath, Tony started counting (5-10-15-20-25...). I bolted straight for my perfect place. When I got there, I climbed over the railing surrounding the staircase that went down to the cellar. I looked back at Tony (50-55-60-65...) and concluded I didn't have time to climb down the stairs (85-90-95...). I decided to jump.

As soon as I let go of the rail. I looked down and saw it—the 2 x 4 lying on top of other old lumber and plywood scraps. It had only had one rusty nail sticking up, but wouldn't you know it—that one nail pierced the bottom of my left tennis shoe. As it entered my foot, I heard Tony say, "HUNDRED! OLLY-OLLY-OXEN-FREE!"

With the hot throbbing pain, I gritted my teeth, so I didn't scream. I stepped on the board with my right foot and yanked my left foot free. I felt immediate relief and thought things were going to be okay. Tony was busy trying to tag Ramon "it," and I saw my chance to reach the tree we used as Home. I put my right foot on the first step and went to set my left foot down on the second. Everything was okay until I put weight on it. That was a bad idea; I tried to make it up the rest of the steps by grabbing the railing and hopping. As I got to the top, Tony saw me and came charging; I lunged to avoid his tag, but to no avail. Now I was "it," AND I had a hole in my foot!

We were all gathered at home base, huffing, and puffing, Cartwright style. In my memory, there were other Maffit kids hanging around, but I can't tell you names or gender. Everyone was yelling to get the game on, 'cause it was gonna be getting dark, and Jacques was it, and Cindy was screaming, "LET'S GO!!!" I really wanted to call the game, but I also didn't want anyone to know I had a very painful wound. I argued that all the good hiding spaces had been found and everybody was tired and…and.

Thankfully, the bells announcing the Ice Cream Man could be heard in the distance. Faster than you could say "ice cream samich" the backyard had emptied. I sat there by myself knowing I couldn't run. Thinking I would be missed, I hobbled out to the curb, but I didn't want any ice cream. Everyone sat on the front porch to eat their frozen goodies, while I just tried to find a position for my foot that didn't hurt so bad. I realized I didn't even know what the hole looked like. I could go to the bathroom, but I would have to limp in front of everybody, and the questions about why was I walking funny would come from a family who were naturally nosy and kids I just met and couldn't name if you paid me. I decided to sit tight till people started wandering off to watch cartoons or whatever. I started imagining the nail hole, and the longer I sat there, the worse it got. I pictured torn flesh, a gaping wound with blood and pus running out of it. The thought almost made me cry, and then I realized I had to pee—bad.

I tried to walk as normally as I could. Every step on my left foot hurt worse than a stroke from a switch off Grandma's tree. And there was a squishiness in my shoe that I guessed was blood. As soon as I was out of everyone's sight, I began hopping on one foot and made it to the bathroom. I took care of the first order of business and then closed the toilet and sat down. I started to take off my shoe, but the pain stopped me cold. Any pressure or twist shot pain right to the wound. I almost decided against yanking the shoe off because, even if the pain was over real quick, I knew I would still have to put it back on. And that would hurt much worse. But, gritting my teeth, I removed my shoe and then my sock. Well, there was some blood, but not as much as I had imagined. I immediately felt better, and I began to figure out how I could survive this ordeal without telling anybody. Maybe if I stayed off my foot for a while, everything would be okay. Maybe I could claim to be sick or have a headache. I could climb in a bed somewhere and just wait it out.

I was looking closely at the wound again and making my plan when I remembered the nail had been dirty and rusty. I could see some swelling, and now the pain was growing worse. Being eight years old, I had no idea what to do. I figured, "How bad could it get? My foot certainly couldn't hurt any more than it already did. I put my shoe back on and tied it very loosely. Man, that hurt, but I got through it.

I emerged bravely from the bathroom and made it to an empty spot on the couch to absent-mindedly watch a combination of afternoon cartoons and old Three Stooges movies. The longer I sat there, the worse the pain got, and the deeper my confusion about what to do. There were only us kids in the house, and I didn't think they would know either. So I just sat there and hurt.

I must have fallen asleep, 'cause the next thing I knew there was a key in the door and everybody was screaming, "Momma's home! Momma's home!" This "Momma" was my Aunt Vanetta. She was my momma's third sister. Vanetta came in the house complaining about how tired she was and how the white folks at her job had gotten on her last nerve. She proclaimed that she was gonna sit down, have a drink and a cigarette, and the kids better shut the hell up and get away from her. These statements made me determined not to tell Aunt Vanetta anything about my foot.

As more time passed, the more miserable I became. Things in the house hadn't settled down at all. The TV was on. There was a radio playing James Brown. Now Vanetta was up and banging pots and pans in the kitchen. Someone was on the phone. Somebody was yelling at somebody else. I wasn't moving an inch if I didn't have to. Suddenly, Vanetta announced dinner. All other activity ceased, and everyone appeared, like magic, at the dinner table. I was the only who had to show up a little late, and the entire Cartwright clan watched me make my way into the dining room. I tried to walk as normally as I could, and truth be told, I thought I was doing a pretty good job. Apparently, I was hallucinating, because Vanetta took one look at my clenched teeth and obviously painful walk and demanded, "WHAT THE HELL HAPPENED TO YOU?"

All the Cartwright kids started gawking at me as if they were seeing me for the first time. "OOOOH!" "DANG!" "I DIDN'T DO NOTHIN'!" I started crying, partly because at least now I could acknowledge the pain, and partly because I was scared that the wrath of Vanetta was about to come down on me. I mumbled something about hurting my foot, and I guess I must have said the word "nail," because that's when she went off. "What nail? What are you talking about!?!"

I stood there, basically on one foot, trying to get the story of playing Hide n' Go Seek and jumping over the rail and seeing the nail and all the rest when I got a good look at Vanetta's face. She was staring at me like I had absolutely no sense. "Why didn't you tell somebody? You ever had a tetanus shot?" To this day I still think that was a funny question to ask an eight-year-old, but she kept talking, saying things I really can't remember now. All the while, the other Cartwright noise continued unabated. The next thing I knew, Vanetta grabbed my hand and swooped me up in the jet stream created whenever Vanetta Cartwright was on a mission.

I don't remember how we got to the hospital, but I do remember that all five of the Cartwright Kids went with us. Homer G. Phillips was a huge institution, built as Negro Hospital #2. In its day, it was the largest training hospital for Black doctors and nurses west of the Mississippi River. Vanetta, like most residents of North St. Louis, was justifiably proud of Homer G. Phillips. Still, having to take a silly-ass nephew to the emergency room after a long day at work was a pain, no matter how you cut it.

Now Vanetta wasn't a big woman, but she cut a wide swath where ever she went. You could say she moved with a purpose. Well, on this night, she was not going to be deterred. When we got to the hospital, I thought someone from the hospital might show up to help. Nope. Vanetta got out of the car and said in a loud voice that defined her exasperation with the situation, "COME ON!" She grabbed me by the wrist and suddenly, I didn't have to worry about walking on my injured foot because I was limply flapping along behind her as she dragged me into the emergency room. The Cartwright Kids paraded along behind us, still interacting more with each other than with anything going on around them. Vanetta sat me down in the waiting area, announced herself at the desk, filled out some paperwork, and then came back and sat next to me. I guess everyone else found seats or sat on the floor or had wheelchair races. This was becoming a bigger deal than I had imagined, and now I was really scared 'cause Vanetta was going to have to tell…my Momma!

Vanetta said, "Are you okay?" I nodded, and she smiled. It was not the sweet Auntie smile that one might expect. It was an "I am gonna talk about you for forty-four years, 'cause this is about the dumbest shit I have ever heard of!" smile. "What the hell were you thinking?" Then she let out a snort and a laugh that was oddly comforting. I was no longer the quiet nephew from Chicago. I was the dumb-ass nephew from Chicago who managed to drive a nail through his foot and lived to tell the tale. Of course, Vanetta told my mother, but it was not nearly the traumatic event I thought it would be. I don't even think the words, 'emergency room' came up. In any event, there wasn't a big to-do about the whole affair. I would dare-say I am the only one who even remembers the day I got that scar, how I got it or the details that seemed so important to me then.

The house on Maffit is a fading part of the Cartwright past. The Cartwright children then have become aunts, uncles, and grandparents. We are the elders now.

Vanetta, Raymond, Clovis, and Momma are all gone. But every time I see that spot on my left foot, I am aware that it represents much more than one little boy's afternoon adventure, and certainly, something that goes far beyond my singular experience. It has become for me a marker on the map of St. Louis and Perkins and Bordeaux family history, an entire people's history, and by extension, true American history. I remember that my Aunt Vanetta was talking to a Negro admitting nurse. The doctor who saw me was Colored. The nurse who gave me the tetanus shot was Black.

In the 1960s, Homer G. Phillips Hospital was an institution in the African American community, built to serve the people in that community. The social forces of segregation and discrimination that defined why that "special" hospital existed did not diminish the pride that community had in the hospital. Homer G. Phillips hospital was a massive civic effort to contain the Black community in the north end of the city; to keep the Black community in its place. Having an all-Black hospital in the Ville meant those patients didn't have to come to hospitals in the southern part of the city. Black doctors didn't have to work across the city. Phillips was a City hospital but simultaneously separate from the other City hospitals. At the same time, it was the Black community's hospital, and that sense of ownership was absolute. I too take a certain amount of pride in being treated at Homer G. Phillips Hospital, even for something as meaningless as stupidly stepping on a rusty nail. For one evening, amidst emergency room ebb and flow, I got to see what an organization staffed exclusively with people of color could accomplish. I carry the legacy of that once-great Ville landmark with me and honor the contributions it made to the city and people of St. Louis.

All that happened half a century ago. The hospital was closed and left dormant for years. It was retrofitted and remodeled and now has a second life as a beautiful retirement community. Our beloved Aunt Juanita, Momma's oldest sister, and the last of the Perkins five sisters, lived there with her husband, Ivan, until he transitioned. I visited them a few times and noticed that I could look across Whittier Avenue and identify the remains of my father's boyhood home and his grandfather's home right next door. The ram-shackle remnants were shotgun houses that held fifteen people between them. Looking at those decaying walls and foundations, I could almost look back in time and see the world of my father and his family. Daddy's six brothers and sisters and his parents would have been in a two-bedroom house that didn't have indoor plumbing until Daddy's father built a bathroom. There were more horses pulling carriages than there were cars on the cobblestone roads. The Ville was a tightly proscribed, segregated district with all of the associated economic and social effects that went along with it. The unintended by-product of this segregation was the excellence of high schools like Charles Sumner and Vashon. There were teachers and nurses and doctors and lawyers and postal workers and every other kind of citizens working and living pretty decent lives, as long as they did not stray from their socially assigned and enforced roles. Looking down on a century of progress and change gave me pause. I wondered why I was chosen to get the blessings that flowed from this particular family tree.

From one of those shotgun houses had sprung seven children, my father being the eldest. He made his way from this environment to Lincoln University, the Minnesota School of Engineering and St. Louis University. He was a Tuskegee Airman and got to work on the world's first atom-splitter at the University of Chicago. He and Momma were married for almost fifty years and raised four sons in turbulent times. He gave my brothers and me what his father and Uncle Don gave him and added a little something to it. I have often tried to identify what it was that Daddy and Momma gave us. The 'something' was all

Clo and Neecy before they became Momma and Daddy.

the blessings that have accrued to me through the years. Daddy and Momma worked hard to put my brothers and me on the solid foundation of a good education. They believed from the very beginning that being literate and well-spoken were assets that could be used in any numbers of ways. The ability to communicate, in written and spoken words, was paramount. But an appreciation for the wider world came in a close second. Daddy had given us that appreciation for the natural world and how everything worked and had aggravated us by his focus and precision. Momma had gifted us the liberal arts; insisted that we played musical instruments and listened to all sorts of music. We saw plays and went to museums to see the world from different perspectives. We read books—not just comics, but classics too—and talked about the social upheaval that surrounded us.

The 'something' was the ability to think critically. I may have made some mistakes in my life, but they were more often errors of immaturity and execution rather than faulty reasoning. Momma and Daddy had a plan for their family, and they were singularly focused, sometimes to almost laughable extremes, on preparing us for a future I don't think either of them could even envision. I once lobbied my mother to let me get out of a typing class in high school. I whined and sniveled about being the only boy in the class and how I was never going to have to know how to type. Momma was adamant. "You'll need to type your term papers." She saw me in college long before I got the idea, and her insistence that I learn to type on an old manual Smith-Corona typewriter with no letters on the keys was about more than term papers. Did she foresee the importance of the keyboard to the futuristic world of computing? I choose to think she glimpsed the future.

The 'something' was a dry and droll sense of humor and a skeptical view of the world. Daddy was a pragmatic realist. Though emotional, Momma was constant. You knew what to expect with both of my parents, and whatever their differences and challenges, they were a united front. There were no surprises with Clo and Neecy. When I was deciding on a major, I had chosen Sociology kind of haphazardly, and when Clovis heard my choice, he hardly reacted but said, "I can't wait for all those sociology companies to start hiring." He wasn't criticizing or belittling my choice, just reminding me to keep an eye on the practical things of life, like earning a living.

I have carried these 'somethings' forward in my life, and Valerie and I have made a pretty good case for passing on a Bordeaux legacy, as well as a Lacy and Murphy legacy on her side of our family. We have tried to add our little 'something' for our kids and now encourage our son to do the same for his two children. The strength and sustenance we get from our different family trees are immeasurable. We know some, though not all of the stories of facing down klansmen and living through the Depression. We have stories of triumph and excellence to go with the tragedies. From my youngest days on the South Side of Chicago through our periodic visits to St. Louis, to our time in Compton and Pomona, I got everything I needed to meet the world from saints along the way like Momma's three surviving sisters. I only detailed a few of them in these pages.

I want to close with this thought: None of us are very successful without at least a little help from our friends. Collaboration and cooperation are essential. Every good thing I have ever accomplished, personally or professionally, I have done with someone else. Often someone way smarter and more talented than I. Education? Check. Employment? Check. Marriage?

Check. Parenthood? Check. Home ownership? Check. Social Awareness? Check. You get my point. I believe in the unity of collaboration and the value of contributing to someone else's life. It is those Saints, in Sintown and elsewhere, that have collaborated in my life, contributed to the man I have become. I am also the link between those Bordeaux's and Perkins that came before us to our children, and now, grandchildren. What I as a man, husband, and father have given my children is the collective 'something's' of my ancestors with my little something added to it. What they do with this legacy and inheritance is beyond my control save to advise and counsel. But it is that little something that gives my kids a firmer foundation from which to begin their lives and building their own legacies.

CPSIA information can be obtained
at www.ICGtesting.com
Printed in the USA
FSHW011737080120
65846FS

9 781977 220042